Business Credit Decoded

Written by: Jeffrey Cater
Edited Formatted and Published by: Jeffrey Cater
First Edition

First Physical Printing: March 2023
E-book Published: March 2023

Introduction

It is estimated that over 90% of the business population knows nothing about business credit. As a result, many business owners use their personal credit for business purposes at great consequence. Over 50% of businesses today fail, and with most of those businesses, the business owner used their personal guarantee for their business debt, costing them their family's entire life savings and personal assets.

With this book in your hands, you are about to become a business credit master. You will know precisely how to build business credit scores and a business credit profile for a business. With this business credit profile created you and your business can obtain large amounts of credit and funding for your business without having to supply a personal guarantee and being personally liable for your business debts.

I have helped over 11,000 clients improve their credit, build business credit, and qualify for financing. I have had the opportunity to witness thousands of loans get underwritten; and seen first-hand how lenders make their lending decisions. I have helped consumers build and repair personal credit to qualify for lending. And I have helped business owners obtain hundreds of millions of dollars in funding. I have dedicated more than a decade to learning everything about how creditors and lenders do business.

That knowledge has helped create one of the most advanced business credit building systems in existence today. This system has been used to support business owners to obtain funding and build business credit for their businesses. These unique business credit building methods are also taught at the most significant credit conventions in the nation to other credit firms. And now this book will give you the knowledge and power to fight and win the business credit battle.

This book is designed to give you a step-by-step process of understanding how to build credit and obtain funding for any business. You will learn first to understand the business credit system itself, then to know what lenders are looking for to approve a company for credit and funding, and, finally, you will learn where to go to secure funding for your business and know about the types of financing available today. Your business can have an excellent credit score and qualify for credit and funding without you having to offer a personal guarantee. This book will show you how.

Table of Contents

The Power of Business Credit

You have definitely heard of Equifax, Experian, Trans Union, and the FICO score before. In the United States these have become household names. On the other hand, most Americans and even most business owners have still never heard of a DUNS number, Paydex score, Intelliscore, or even Dun and Bradstreet.

Entrepreneur.com reported that fewer than 10% of business owners have any knowledge whatsoever of business credit. This is great news for you, because now that you are reading this book you do know about, and will thoroughly understand, the power of business credit. What's more, that means that the other 90% of business owners know nothing about business credit, leaving more money available for the smaller percentage who do – including, now, you.

Most business owners quickly get accustomed to using their personal credit as personal guarantee for their businesses. As a result, most never realize that it is possible to obtain considerable credit for their business with no personal guarantee or personal credit inquiry – hence, with no personal risk.

Business Credit bases approvals on the credit profile and score of the business, not its owner. The business owner's personal credit profile is not reviewed at all, because it's their business profile that is used to determine approval. The business is approved for credit, not the owner, meaning that in many cases there is no personal guarantee required.

Personal Guarantee

Most business owners currently use credit with a Personal Guarantee (PG). A personal guarantee is an agreement that makes the business owner in person liable for the business's debts and or obligations. With a personal guarantee, in the case of a default the creditor can pursue the personal home, bank accounts, investments, and file judgments against assets of the business owners in person. No PG means the business takes on the risk, not the business owner. This keeps their personal finances safe and secure.

One of the most common mistakes entrepreneurs make is using personal credit to finance their businesses. A recent study showed that 87% of ALL businesses mix personal and business credit. Common examples include paying for business expenses with personal credit cards and obtaining personal loans to finance business expenses.

There are several severe, adverse effects on the business owner who does this when an owner personally guarantees business-related financing, the lender will require a personal credit check.

Every time an inquiry appears on an individual's credit history, his or her personal credit score takes are lowered. The lower the score, the harder it is to secure financing, and the more interest is charged.

A further adverse effect of the business owner using their personal credit for business debts is that the more personal credit is used to guarantee a business, the higher the business owner's debt-to-income ratio will be. This means that in future financing lenders will only be willing to give less money. This obviously impacts on the individual's personal life. Signing that loan for the business could prevent the business owner from getting a mortgage or a personal car loan.

When a business owner uses their personal resources or credit to finance a business, they chain their financial security to their company's success. If the company fails, the business owner is then left holding the bag, and their personal finances will be ruined along with their business. This reality is very practical, particularly considering that over 50% of businesses now fail in the first 3 years, largely due to a lack of access to capital.

Each time personal assets are pledged for any type of credit extended to a business, the business owner jeopardizes their personal assets, including savings and investment accounts, cars, even their home. If the business can't pay off its debt, the bank will come looking for them *personally* to make good on the loan. It doesn't matter if the owner owns 25% or 100% of the business, the lender can pursue the person who supplied the personal guarantee for the entire business debt.

A business entity established as a sole proprietorship is most susceptible to this risk. Although the owner can build business credit as a sole proprietor, they will be completely liable for all personal and corporate debt.

Their credit history will be based solely on activity associated with their social security number because they will not have a corporate tax ID number. As a sole proprietor, they also have no legal means for separating corporate and personal credit.

The best way to protect personal assets is to incorporate the business. Having done so, business owners can then shield themselves from personal liability for the company's debts and will typically also reduce their tax burden. Many business owners are unaware of the value of incorporation. Even fewer understand the essential steps necessary for building the kind of corporate credit that will enable them to take full advantage of their entrepreneurial status.

Incorporation makes the business entity separate from the business owner, a separate entity with its own liability. Incorporation separates business assets from the business owner's personal assets. If someone decides to sue the company, they cannot touch the business owner's house, car, or anything else owned by them or their family.

By incorporating the business, the business is also enabled to begin establishing corporate credit, which will ultimately provide the funds needed to grow the business and one day get to the point where the business can obtain funding without a personal guarantee.

Financial Mistakes

Business owners typically are making big financial mistakes when it comes to business credit. One of the big mistakes is having the business not building business and financial credibility by building business credit. Another serious issue is the business owner contaminating personal credit and business credit by using personal credit for business debts.

Investing personal credit and cash into the business without reporting to credit agencies is another big financial mistake many business owners make. They do have trade credit, but that credit doesn't end up reporting to the business credit reporting agencies and thereby allowing their business to build credit.

Using personal credit cards, cash, line of credit, etc. to pay business expenses is another big problem business owners are susceptible to. This creates a big financial issue, as the business owner puts the family assets at risk of business debts. When this happens, the business owner is creating personal liability by pledging personal assets rather than utilizing corporate credit.

Another major financial mistake business owners make is not paying their bills on time. In many cases this lowers the business credit scores, making it harder to get new credit at good terms. Most business owners also don't manage their business credit as they should, as an asset rather than a liability.

A lot of business owners don't realize that business credit is an asset that grows with the business. But personal credit has a predetermined limit and borrowing ceiling, limiting what the business owner can be approved for. Building a strong business credit profile will help the business cash flow by reducing or improving vendor and supplier terms, credit card rates, financing costs and insurance premiums.

There are many questions a business owner should ask to know if building business credit makes sense for them.

- Have I ever ***been declined*** for a business loan or financing?
- Could I use a business ***line of credit*** for working capital?
- Do I need, now or in the forseeable future, to ***lease equipment?***
- Am I currently stuck having to ***personally guarantee*** every loan?
- Would I like to obtain easy, fast approval on credit cards for my business?
- Do I currently receive the most favorable credit terms from vendors?

There's an unfortunate lack of useful information available on how to finance a business, especially when it comes to building business credit that will allow a business owner to finance, operate and expand the business without putting their personal finances, or their family's very future, in jeopardy.

When a business owner applies for credit for a business, most creditors will pull the business credit report. This credit might have been used for anything in the business from credit cards, to loans, to equipment, even to auto loans.

When a lender pulls a business credit report and there is nothing there, they'll rely on the business owner's personal credit to guarantee the financing. And if there's no business credit file, they're not able to lend as much credit to the business as they would an established business credit profile. One of the main reasons a business owner needs a business credit report is the ability to receive more funding.

One of the most important reasons it makes sense to build business credit is to save money. By building business credit, a business owner can save themselves and their business money.

Building a strong business credit rating is vitally important to business success. Without it, the business owner will pay much more (at higher interest rates) for the money they borrow, if they can get approved at all. In fact, banks, which say they want to help small business owners; in fact, they turn down over 97% of all business loan applications. They don't make it easy for a business to get approved.

Let's look at a quick example. Let's suppose that a business needs $50,000 for a necessary piece of equipment. Without a strong business credit rating, their bank will only use the business owner's personal credit as a reference. If they get approved, they'll get (in this example) an interest rate of 18%. With a D&B report, that business can lower the interest rate to perhaps 10%, with the business owner not having to guarantee the loan with their personal assets.

To see a quick comparison of the above scenario, see Figure 1.

	Personal Loan	**Business Loan**
Lease Amount	$50,000	$50,000
Interest Rate	18%	10%
Term of Lease	60 months	60 months
Monthly Payment	$1,269.67	$1,062.35
Total Payments	$76,180.20	$63,741.00
Total Savings		***$12,439.20***

Figure 1

By simply building business credit and setting up a business properly, the business owner can literally save tens of thousands of dollars. When it comes to the bottom line, business owners must pay close attention to these kinds of savings.

It doesn't matter how long a business has been in business – one year, five years, even twenty years. As far as the banks are concerned, if that business doesn't have a business credit rating, they are only going to lend a personal loan, with personal guarantees required for the business owner.

This creates multiple issues, as the average consumer credit report gets just one inquiry per year and has 11 credit obligations, typically broken down as 7 credit cards and 4 installment loans. Business owners are not your average consumer because they carry both personal and business credit. This typically doubles the number of inquiries made to their personal credit profile and the number of credit obligations they carry at any given time, all of which negatively impact their personal credit score.

Beyond that, because business inquiries and personal inquiries aren't separated on their personal credit report, their scores are, again, negatively affected. At the same time, by using their personal credit history to get business credit, they're not able to build their business score, which could help them attain critical business credit in the future. The key to establishing a business credit profile and score is to find companies that will establish credit for your business.

Business Credit Basics

Business credit gives entrepreneurs a unique opportunity to build, maintain and acquire credit, both individually and for their business. That means business owners can build and grow their companies without having to rely solely on their personal credit.

In the United States, when a consumer with a social security number accepts their first job or applies for their first credit card, a credit profile is started with the personal credit reporting agencies.

This profile is consistently added to, with credit inquiries, new employment and address changes, new credit accounts, and other public record data. Eventually, the credit report becomes a statement of an individual's ability to pay back a debt.

In many cases, the same is true for businesses. When a business issues another business credit, it's referred to as trade credit. Trade or business credit is the single largest source of lending in the world.

Information about trade credit transactions is gathered by the business credit bureaus to create a business credit report using the business name, address, and federal tax identification number (FIN), also known as an employer identification number (EIN), issued by the Internal Revenue Service.

The business credit bureaus use this compiled data to generate a report about the company's business credit transactions. In many cases, those issuing credit to will rely on the business credit report to determine whether they want to grant credit to the business, and if so, how much and at what terms.

To qualify for most business credit sources, the business must have a positive credit score established with the appropriate business credit reporting agencies. The major business credit bureaus that compile and provide copies of the reports are Dun & Bradstreet, Experian Business, and Equifax Business.

Once a positive business credit score is established, many merchants will then approve the business owner for credit in the business's name. Thousands of major merchants offer business credit. But most don't promote their business credit programs, so they are difficult to locate. Some merchants offering business credit include Chevron, Dell, Staples, Lowes, Visa, MasterCard, even large banks like Wells Fargo and Bank of America.

Once business credit is established and paid-as-agreed, the business credit scores will continue to increase. As more positive credit history is established and scores increase, business owners can then be approved for even more credit with higher credit limits.

With business credit the business can even qualify for loans, credit lines, auto financing, even mortgages with business credit established. Business credit is an outstanding resource for businesses. Owners can obtain credit to run and expand their businesses without the personal liability of using a personal guarantee.

Currently, information provided to the business credit bureaus is sent in voluntarily. No business is required to send it in. Therefore, in the case of most businesses, the credit bureaus never receive all or even any information. Many companies go years growing their business credit without any of it being reported to the credit bureaus.

Because of the lack of reporting and promotion of business credit by the credit industry, many entrepreneurs are not at all familiar with business credit. Due to this unfamiliarity, many myths have been formed relating to business credit.

Business Credit Myths

In some ways, a business has many of the same attributes as an individual person. Businesses earn income and file tax returns, debtors are paid, credit is used for the business, and many businesses have credit histories.

Still, some business owners overlook the importance of a healthy business credit profile and score or don't know anything about business credit at all. Because of this, many business owners start believing the myths surrounding business credit instead of the real facts.

One of the myths about business credit is that the credit isn't real credit with real merchants, or creditors. The reason for this myth is that although most major merchants offer business credit, most do not promote the fact that they offer it.

There is no reason for a company to advertise they have credit where the applicant has no personal liability. For instance, Home Depot offers a commercial credit account. But in almost all cases, the applicant must be willing to provide their social security number when applying and is willing to take on the personal guarantee for the debt.

So, it doesn't make sense for Home Depot to then offer the applicant a card with no personal liability if the applicant is willing to sign and give that guarantee and accept the liability. Yet Home Depot does offer business credit with no personal guarantee, even though they don't advertise it.

Many merchants are the same: they offer business credit but don't promote the fact that they offer it. Business credit with no personal credit check or guarantee is available through Lowes, Home Depot, Office Max, Staples, BP, Shell, Wal-Mart, Sam's Club, Costco, Radio Shack, and thousands of other major merchants. But you'd never know it if you didn't look into it carefully.

Another myth is that business credit limits and loan amounts are smaller than consumer credit. Credit limits on business credit accounts are notably higher than consumer cards. A business owner can secure credit cards with $10,000 limits even after having a business credit score for only a few months. This is impossible to accomplish with personal credit.

And with 5-10 accounts reporting on the business credit report, a business owner can qualify for multitudes of business credit cards with limits of $10,000 or higher. A business owner can build massive amounts of business credit much, much faster than consumer credit. And the interest rates and incentives are similar, if not better on corporate credit than consumer credit.

There has been much news recently about the record incentives that corporate credit cards are currently offering business owners. These incentives are so good that corporate credit commonly has higher limits and better terms than most consumer credit accounts.

Another business credit myth is that if a company pays all its bills on time, its credit history is strong and in good standing. Unfortunately, while paying bills on time is important, your timely payments only help your credit rating when your business works with creditors who report the payments to business credit reporting agencies.

The secret to business credit is to locate and work with the vendors and merchants who work with the appropriate business credit reporting agencies. Over 90% of trade-credit is not reported to the business reporting agencies. So even if you have many accounts set up with vendors, you still might not have a business credit score, or profile established.

The bottom line with business credit is that as a business owner, you can review the credit standing of your own business and take steps to strengthen or build your corporate credit file and obtain credit with no personal guarantee or credit check.

Business Credit Benefits

Success in business will often be determined by whether the business has an established business credit profile and score. With a good business credit profile, the business will have near-unlimited borrowing power. Lacking having a good business credit profile, it will find a difficult path to success, not having access to working capital and funding.

Therefore, according to Dun & Bradstreet, a strong business credit file can be the difference between receiving business funds or not. Another reason for this is that approval for most small business loan decisions under $90,000 happen automatically and electronically, often relying solely on the established business credit file and score.

Building business credit can improve business cash flow by reducing direct costs associated with financing costs, insurance premiums, vendor and supplier terms, rental terms and credit card rates. Business owners save money with lower interest rates on business loans. And they qualify for more loans, leases, and government contracts.

Business credit eliminates the business owner's personal liability and risk in obtaining financing. It also separates the personal and business credit profiles so that both can be built to obtain greater amounts of credit.

Business credit adds more value to a business and gives the business genuine business credibility. Stakeholders, partners, lenders, even potential buyers of the business will see more value if a strong business credit profile is built.

Therefore, almost all Fortune 500 companies use their business credit to secure funding. It's not that they need the money to operate. Successful companies use funding as leverage to grow their business.

One of the many benefits of business credit is that funding can be obtained with no personal credit check at all. Faced with a strong business credit profile, lenders will lend money based on the business's credit, not the business owners. This is excellent if the owner has personal credit issues, as they will still qualify for funding despite this impediment in their private life.

Even with exceptional personal credit, business credit gives the business owner double the borrowing power. They can get approved for much more credit and higher funding amounts using business credit than they would if they used their personal credit to qualify.

Business Credit Reporting Agencies

There are three major companies that collect business information and publish it. These are Dun & Bradstreet, Experian, and Business Equifax. D&B is by far the largest, but the other two are catching up quickly. Most lending institutions incorporate the information and use the commercial scoring model that they retrieve from D&B's database.

There are a few other business credit reporting companies, but they're not big players and a business owner won't need to worry too much about them. These include PayNet, FDInsight, BusinessCreditUSA, and ClientChecker.

Dun & Bradstreet is the most common and is used by most vendors to extend lines of credit. Landlords use them to approve office leases as well. Experian is used by many credit card companies and non-traditional business lenders. Equifax is called the "Small Business Financial Exchange" and is the most important for cash lenders such as banks. To concentrate on one and not the others is to have lopsided credibility. A business needs to build business credit with all three of these major credit reporting agencies to achieve genuine credibility.

Dun and Bradstreet

Dun and Bradstreet is the biggest and major business credit reporting agency.

Commonly known as D&B, the agency provides information on businesses and corporations for use in credit decisions. Dun and Bradstreet is a publicly traded company with a headquarters in Short Hills New Jersey, and trades on the New York Stock Exchange.

D&B currently holds the largest supply worldwide of business information, with over 200 million business records on file. In 2012 D&B reported that 129.4 million of these records referred to active companies that were available for risk, supply, sales and marketing decisions. Another 76.7 million were inactive companies, providing historical information for file matching and data cleansing.

Dun & Bradstreet has a massive presence worldwide. Of the over 2 million records they had on file in 2012, they reported 54,409,439 were from Europe while only 33,282,653 were from North America. Another 12,097,055 records were from Latin America, while only 27,451,196 records were from Asia Pacific. The lowest volume of records on file was in Africa, with only 1,184,582 records on file, and the Middle East, with only 1,008,477 records on file.

Altogether, Dun & Bradstreet reported holding 206,148,055 records in January 2012. They also reported having over 1 billion in payment and bank experiences. And they reported over 159 million public records on file.

D&B roots can be tracked all the way back to 1841, with the formation of the Mercantile Agency in New York. In 1933 the Mercantile Agency joined with R.G. Dun & Company and became known as Dun and Bradstreet. In 1962 D&B created the DUNS number, currently the preferred method worldwide of identifying businesses.

Dun & Bradstreet offers many products and services to consumers and business. Some of these include risk management products such as the Business Information Report, Comprehensive Report and the DNBi platform. These provide current and historical business information, primarily used by lenders and financial institutions to assist in making credit decisions.

D&B also offers sales and marketing products such as the DUNS Market Identifier Database, Optimizer, and D&B Professional Contacts, all of which provide sales and marketing professionals with business data for both prospecting and CRM activity.

Just as Equifax, Experian, and Trans Union are leaders in the consumer credit reporting arenas, Dun and Bradstreet is the leader in business credit data.

Dun & Bradstreet has a proprietary DUNSRight Quality Process providing quality business information that is the foundation of their global risk solutions worldwide. The DUNSRight process was created on the basis of four fundamental questions: is the data accurate; is the data complete; is the data timely; and is the data globally consistent.

To answer these questions, Dun & Bradstreet runs data through a process called DUNSRight, in which data is collected, aggregated, edited, and verified via thousands of sources daily. Their ability to turn massive data streams into high-quality business information is one of many factors that set them apart from any other competitor.

D&B first collects data from a variety of sources worldwide. This data is then integrated into their database through their very own patented entity matching system. By applying the D-U-N-S Number and using corporate linkage they enable customers to view their total risk or opportunity across related businesses. D&B then uses predictive indicators to rate businesses' past performance and to access future risk.

They are the leading provider of risk managements, business information, sales and marketing, and supply management decisions worldwide.

A Dun & Bradstreet office in Center Valley PA built in 2006

Experian

Experian was formerly a division of TRW, an automotive electronics giant. TRW was originally founded in 1901 as the Cleveland Cap Screw Company. They started producing screws and bolts and grew to produce many parts for the aviation and automobile industry.

In the early 1960s, TRW started a consumer credit information bureau, collecting and selling consumer data, and eventually became known as TRW Information Systems. TRW Information Systems continued compiling data and were the first to start offering consumers direct credit report access in 1986. In 1991, rampant problems started appearing with TRW reported credit data.

Thousands of people in a town in Vermont had tax liens inaccurately reporting against them. Similar cases started appearing in the entire northeast, forcing the deletion of countless tax liens across the states of Vermont, Rhode Island, New Hampshire, and Maine

Dozens of lawsuits were filed against TRW, claiming sloppy procedures to create credit files, lack of response to consumer complaints, and re-reporting previously deleted incorrect data. All cases were settled out of court.

TRW then created a database known as the Constituent Relations Information Systems (CRIS). This system's sole purpose was to gather personal data on 8,000 politicians who held opinions on TRW.

In 1996, TRW was purchased from Bain Capital and the Tohomas H. Lee Partners for over 1 billion dollars by GUS plc, a private group of investors. It was then combined with CCN, the largest credit reporting company in the United Kingdom. GUS retained the Experian name for their combined credit services subsidiary.

In 2004 Experian continued its growth, purchasing CheetahMail, a business founded in 1998 offering e-mail marketing software and services. In 1998 Experian also acquired QAS, a supplier of contact data management and identity verification solutions. As a result of their growth, Experian became the first company ever to win the UK Business of the Year award twice, winning in both 2003 and 2005.

Experian continued to grow in 2005 with its purchase of PriceGrabber for 485 million dollars. In 2005 Experian also acquired FootFall, an information provider for the real estate and retail property industries. Experian also spent $330 million in 2005 acquiring LowerMyBills.com.

In 2006 Experian made a big move when it announced its purchase of Northern Credit Bureaus, located in Québec, Canada. That same year Experian demerged from their British company GUS plc and was independently listed on the London Stock Exchange.

Since 2005 Experian has continued to aggressively grow their corporation. In 2007 they purchased a 65% stake in Serasa, a leading credit bureau in Brazil, now the largest credit bureau in the world. Experian continued to purchase software companies that year, including Emailing Solution, Hitwise, and Tallyan.

In 2010 Experian became the first CICRA licensed credit bureau to go live in India, where it continues to supply reports to the Reserve Bank of India's (RBI) guidelines.

Currently, Experian continues to grow at a rapid pace. In 2011 they acquired a majority stake in Computec S.A., a credit services provider in Columbia. They also purchased Medical Present Value, Virid Interatividade Digital Ltd., and Garlik Ltd, expanding their data and marketing reach.

Experian has also become the second largest reporting agency in the business credit world. They provide business credit evaluations for over 27,000,000 small businesses and corporations worldwide. These business records are spread over 80 countries that Experian services. Experian's reach is across four main geographic regions, including North America, Latin America, UK and Ireland, and EMEA/ Asia Pacific.

Experian's headquarters are in Dublin, Ireland. They have operational headquarters in Nottingham (UK), Costa Mesa (California), and São Paulo (Brazil). Experian plc is listed on the London Stock Exchange (EXPN) and in a constituent of the FTSE 100 Index. In March 2011 Experian claimed revenue for the prior year of $4.2 million. Currently, Experian employs over 15,000 people, working in 41 countries.

Experian's main business focus is on credit information services. These services provide insight and tolls that help businesses target new markets, predict and manage risk, and optimize customer relationships. Experian also offers Decision Analytics, which enable organizations with large customer bases to manage and automate large volumes of day-to-day decisions. Experian's clients include international banks, utility companies, public service providers, and more.

Experian focuses on providing quality data and analytics to businesses to help them better assess risk. They possess a massive consumer and commercial database that they manage to help businesses obtain the best and most up-to-date information. They then extract significant extra value with this data by applying their own proprietary analytics and software.

Experian diligently works to maintain their worldwide notoriety and growth. Their main global focus is to increase their global reach by expanding their global network and extending their capabilities into new geographic areas. They focus on innovation and on enhancing their analytics to deliver high value to their clients. They also strive to achieve operational excellence by leveraging their global scale to deploy global products into new markets.

Equifax

Equifax is the oldest and largest credit bureau in existence today. They were originally founded in 1898, 70 years before the creation of TransUnion.

Two brothers, Cator and Guy Woolford, created the company. Cator got the idea from his grocery business, where he collected customers' names and evidence of credit worthiness. He then sold that list to other merchants to offset his own business costs.

The success of this tactic led Cator and his attorney brother, Guy, to Atlanta, where they set up what would become one of the most powerful industries in existence today.

The Retail Credit Company was born, and local grocers quickly started using the Woolford service, which expanded rapidly. By the early 1900s the service had expanded from grocers to the insurance industry.

Retail Credit Company continued to grow into one of the largest credit bureaus, by the 1960s having nearly 300 branches in operation. They collected all kinds of consumer data, even rumors about people's marital lives and childhoods. They were also scrutinized for selling this data to just about anyone who would buy it.

Throughout the 60s Equifax continued to provide credit reporting services, but the majority of their business came from making reports to insurance companies when people applied for new insurance policies, including life, auto, fire, and medical insurance. Almost all major insurance companies were using RCC to get information on the health, habits, morals, finances and vehicle use of potential insurees.

Equifax also provided companies with services including investigating insurance claims and making employment reports when people were seeking new jobs. Back in the 60s most of Equifax's credit work was actually being done by their subsidiary, Retailers Commercial Agency.

In the late 60s, Equifax started to compile their data onto computers, giving many more companies access to this data – if they chose to purchase it. They also continued to buy up many more of their smaller competitors, becoming larger and also attracting the attention of the Federal government. They began to earn a bad reputation for selling data to anyone who wanted it, whether or not the data was accurate.

Equifax was gathering details about people including their marital troubles, jobs, school history childhood, sex life, political activates, and more. There was no limit to the kind or amount of data they were collecting. Some of the information was factual, while large swathes of the rest were completely false; some information was literally no more than rumors. Equifax was even said to reward their employees for finding the most negative information about consumers.

In response, when the US Congress met in 1971 it enacted the Fair Credit Reporting Act. This new law was the first to govern the information credit bureaus and regulate what they were allowed to collect and sell. Equifax was no longer allowed to misrepresent itself when conducting consumer investigations and employees were no longer given bonuses on the basis of the negative information they were collecting, the standard practice in the past.

Retail Credit Division was charged with violating this law a few years later, causing even more government restrictions to be implemented. Scarred with a bad reputation for violations of the new credit laws, the company changed its name to Equifax in 1975 to improve its image.

Throughout the 1980s, Equifax, Experian and TransUnion split up the remaining smaller credit rating agencies between them, adding 104 of those to Equifax's portfolio. Equifax aggressively grew throughout the US and Canada, and then began growing their commercial business division across the UK. At this time Equifax started competing more aggressively with rivals Dun & Bradstreet and Experian. They then continued to grow, taking aligning with CSC Credit Services and another 65 additional bureaus.

The insurance reporting aspect of Equifax's model was phased out. At one stage the company also had a division selling specialist credit information to the insurance industry, but they spun off this service, including the Comprehensive Loss Underwriting Exchange (CLUE) database, as ChoicePoint in 1997. Choice Point formerly offered digital certification services, which it sold to Geo Trust in September 2001.

Also, in 2001 Equifax spun off its payment services division, forming the publicly listed company Certegy, which acquired Fidelity National Information Services in 2006. Certegy effectively became a subsidiary of Fidelity National Financial as a result of this reverse acquisition merger. In October 2010 Equifax also acquired Anakam, an identity verification software company.

Equifax has continued to grow, now maintaining over 401 million consumer credit records worldwide. They also expanded their services to direct consumer credit monitoring in 1999. Today Equifax is based in Atlanta, Georgia, and has employees in 14 countries. They are listed as a public company on the New York Stock Exchange (NYSE) under the sign EFX.

Since its inception, Equifax has operated in the business-to-business sector, selling consumer credit and insurance reports and related analytics to a wide array of businesses worldwide. Equifax reports are still commonly used by retailers, insurance firms, healthcare providers, utilities, government agencies, banks, credit unions, personal finance companies, and other financial institutions.

Equifax provides business credit evaluations for small businesses and corporations, allowing them to detect early signs of trouble by monitoring key customers, suppliers & partners. Equifax offers a business scoring credit scoring model known as the Equifax Small Business Enterprise. Equifax's model is designed for companies that provide goods and services to small businesses.

Equifax sells business credit reports, analytics, demographic data, and software. Its reports still provide large amounts of detailed information on the personal credit and payment history of individuals and businesses to indicate how they have honored financial obligations.

Equifax's source of data today is still some of the most vital information used by credit grantors to decide what sort of products or services they offer to their customers and at what terms. Equifax's system for collecting data is NCTUE, an exchange of non-credit data including consumer payment history on Telco and other utility account.

Since 1999 Equifax has also been aggressively growing in several other credit-related areas. It has excelled with their credit fraud and identity theft prevention products. Equifax has also started earning a major part of its revenue from services which provide consumers and businesses with credit monitoring.

Today Equifax is one of the major credit reporting agencies used in many countries. Some of the countries where Equifax is mainly used include Canada, Chile, India, Mexico, Peru, the United Kingdom, and the United States.

Business Credit Score

A business credit score is a mathematical model that is used to depict a business's risk of defaulting on an account within the next 12 months. Business credit scores reflect the likelihood that a customer will pay the merchant back as agreed. Merchants use business credit scores to help them make decisions as to who to lend money to and at what interest rate and terms.

Business credit scores are very different from personal credit scores, for many reasons. Firstly, a business credit score reflects the business's likelihood of defaulting on an obligation, not the business owners. Most business owners have their own consumer credit scores established. Their business also has its own score, based on how the business obligations are being paid.

Consumer and business credit scores also differ in their fundamental makeup. Consumer credit scores outline a consumer's risk of going 90 days late on an obligation within the next 24 months. Business credit scores reflect the business's risk of going 90 days late on an obligation within the next 12 months.

Consumer credit scores range from 350-850, with 850 being the best. Credit scores of 800 and above are considered excellent credit. Scores of 700 and above are typically considered good credit while scores of 600 reflect average credit. Consumer credit scores of 500 reflect below average credit and scores of 400 or less reflect poor credit.

Consumer scores have five main components. Each of these components carries a different percentage of the overall credit score makeup. The largest aspect of the score relates to payment history, which accounts for 35% of the overall credit score.

With consumer credit scoring, the consumer's available credit or their use of their accounts is the second largest score factor, affecting 30% of the overall score. The length of time the credit file has been open for accounts for 15% of the overall score. The credit mix and the amount of new credit that the consumer is applying for each account for 10% of the overall consumer credit score.

Business credit scores typically range from 0-100, with 100 being the best. Business credit scores are based on one factor only: whether or not the business pays its obligations on time. The business's score directly reflects how that business pays.

Payment Expectation	Credit Score
Expect payment may come early	100
Payments are in early discount period	90
Payment is prompt	80
Payment comes 14 days beyond terms	70
Payment comes 21 days beyond terms	60
Payment comes 30 days beyond terms	50
Payment comes 60 days beyond terms	40
Payment comes 90 days beyond terms	30
Payment comes 120 days beyond terms	20
Unavailable	UN

There are three main agencies offering business credit profiles and scores. These agencies all have their own unique credit scoring formula. Despite their differences, most of their score ranges remain between 0-100. The three reporting agencies who are best known for offering business credit risk scores are the previously discussed Dun & Bradstreet, Experian, and Equifax.

Dun & Bradstreet

The main credit score used in the business world is known as a Paydex score, provided by Dun and Bradstreet. The exact definition from Dunn& Bradstreet (D&B) is: "The D&B PAYDEX® Score is D&B's unique dollar-weighted numerical indicator of how a firm paid its bills over the past year, based on trade experiences reported to D&B by various vendors".

The Paydex score ranges from 0-100, with 100 being the best score a business can obtain. A score of 80 or higher is considered "good" or healthy credit. A business can obtain a good business Paydex credit score by ensuring payments are made promptly to suppliers and vendors.

D&B also offers a predictive credit score, the Supplier Evaluation Risk Rating (SER). This rating predicts the likelihood that a company will file for bankruptcy and cease operations within the next 12 months. This score ranges from 1-9, with 1 being the lowest risk and 9 being the highest.

D&B's other supplier risk score is the Supplier Stability Indicator (SSI). This model predicts the likelihood that a supplier will encounter a large and significant financial or operational stress over the next 90 days. This score ranges from 0-10 with 0 being the lowest risk and 10 the highest.

Every business must first have a D.U.N.S number before Dun & Bradstreet will assign a Paydex score. The Data Universal Numbering System (DUNS) is a business identifier code provided by Dun and Bradstreet. This business identifier code was developed in 1963 to support Dun and Bradstreet's credit reporting practices.

Today the DUNS number is widely used to identify businesses lending for issuing new credit. It is also used by the European Commission, United Nations, and the United States government. More than 50 global, industry, and trade associations recognize, recommend, or require DUNS. The DUNS database now contains over 100 million entries for businesses throughout the world.

The DUNS number is a nine-digit number issued by Dun & Bradstreet and assigned to each business location in the D&B database, each having a unique, separate, and distinct operation for the purpose. The DUNS number is a randomly assigned number used to identify the business.

Unlike national Employment Identification Number (EIN), a DUNS number may be issued to any business worldwide. Certain U.S. government agencies require that a vendor have a DUNS number as well as a U.S. Employer Identification Number (EIN).

The Office of Management and Budget, a United States federal agency, announced in the June 27, 2003 issue of the Federal Register (68 FR 38402) that a DUNS number would be required for all grant applicants for new or renewal awards submitted on or after October 1, 2003.

The DUNS number supplements other identifiers, such as the EIN, and is required whether the application is made electronically or on paper. Other agencies, such as some United Nations offices and Australian government agencies, require certain businesses to have a DUNS number. A DUNS number is also a way in which separate corporate entities, having no official relationship, can be branded as one by sharing a single DUNS number among the affiliated companies.

A DUNS number is sometimes formatted with embedded dashes to promote readability, such as 15-048-3782. Modern usage typically omits dashes and shows the number in the form 150483782. The dashes are not part of D&B's official definition of the DUNS number.

Numerous other business numbering systems exist independent of DUNS—for example, the International Suppliers Network system. However, few, if any, register as many international businesses as DUNS. Today the Dun and Bradstreet's unique DUNS number is the most widely used worldwide method of identifying businesses.

Dun & Bradstreet credit reports provide access to the Paydex score and a great deal of other valuable information. The business's name, address, and phone number are on each report, along with the business's history, including incorporation date, shares of business owners, and even information on directors, including resume details. D&B also lists any affiliations with that business and other businesses, other branches, even subsidiaries.

D&B reports also include financial information such as known sales for the company and net worth (if known). They list the financial condition of the company, their own rating, the DUNS number, and a breakdown of what the Paydex score represents along with the actual score.

Dun & Bradstreet further lists in their reports details on payments the business has made for each individual account, including their full payment record, their upper-credit limit, how much they currently owe on each account, how much is past due, what the terms of the account are, and when the account was reported and last updated.

Extra information S&B provides includes detailed financial information for the business. This information might include current assets, liabilities, working capital, net worth, sales, new profit and loss, and more. D&B will even detail the actual assets and liabilities if these are known. Also included in D&B reports are public record information, including judgments, bankruptcies, other public filings, other liens, UCC filings, and government activity for that business.

D&B reports also list payment details for each account. They also add detailed commentary to the report indicating payment patterns. The term "Antic" indicates that payments are typically received prior to date of invoice (Anticipated). The term "Disc" means payments are received within the trade discount period (Discount). The term "Ppt" indicates that payments are received within terms granted (Prompt). "Slow" confirms that payments are beyond vendor's terms and are being paid late. The term "Ppt-Slow" indicates that some invoices are paid within terms, while others are paid beyond terms. The symbol **(#)** indicates that no manner of payment was provided. And some accounts even provide payment commentary such as "credit refused" or "cash advance".

One of the most important sections of the D&B Business Credit Report is the payment summary section. There are two scores in this section that are critical to the report and can separate a good report from a bad one. While the two scores – the PAYDEX score and the PAYDEX score key – are related, they deal with separate issues that the business owner needs to know and understand.

The PAYDEX score is a statistical measure of your business creditworthiness, basically the business's ability to pay its debts, very similar to a person's personal creditworthiness. A PAYDEX score of 80 is similar to that of a 700 personal FICO credit score.

A business will need a PAYDEX score of 80 to obtain the most favorable financing. This score simply reflects the business pay all bills on time. To obtain a PAYDEX score, a business will need at least five trade accounts reporting to their file. The business credit score itself is calculated by using as many as 875 payments.

It is important for a business owner to have those accounts report favorable payment history. If bills are paid on time, the business credit score will be positive. But if payments are made late, the PAYDEX business credit score will drop. The PAYDEX score will adjust according to how early or late the bills are paid, if bills are paid, then that business can achieve a score that is over 80.

How timely bills are paid (the main indicator of the PAYDEX score) is a good indicator to lenders of how likely that business is to pay its bills at an agreed-upon date in the future. Lenders look at this score carefully when deciding whether or not to give a business a loan.

Another important aspect of the Paydex system of which most business owners are aware is a Paydex "weighted average" score. This score gives more weight to the trade accounts that report higher amounts of credit extended and less weight to trade accounts that are reporting lower dollar amounts of credit.

This leads to a great tip. If a business owner is having any trouble "meeting all their credit payback obligations", in other words if they know they are going to have to pay a bill late, it is important for that business to be sure to pay the "largest dollar" creditors first. This way, their reporting, which carries more weight in the business Paydex score, will remain positive.

If this scenario does come about, it is always best for the business owner to contact those creditors they can't pay and let them know that they are not being ignored.

The business owner should let the creditor know that they have hit a snag and will make it up to them as soon as possible, preferably even giving a date for payment. From a creditor's point of view, the only thing worse than not being paid what's owed to you is not even being told that you're not being paid what's owed to you.

Experian

Experian's business credit scoring model is designed for companies that provide goods and services to small businesses. Experian's business model has many names but is best known as Intelliscore. This model is the second most commonly used in the business world today and is growing rapidly in popularity.

Experian's most recent score system is known as Intelliscore Plus, which they boast of as the next level in credit scoring. This method was released in 2008. Intelliscore Plus considers hundreds of variables to offer a business score between 0-100, with 100 being the highest.

The 0-100 is a percentile score that reflects the percentage of businesses that score higher or lower than the specific business being looked at. For example, if the business has a score of 20, this means that company scores better than 19% of other businesses. That also means that 80% of other businesses score higher than that business.

Intelliscore Plus is advertised as a highly predictive score that provides a very detailed and accurate reflection of a business's risk. Intelliscore actually predicts a business's risk of going seriously delinquent, or over 91 days late, or having a major financial issue such as bankruptcy within the next 12 months.

Intelliscore is already being widely used. Many of the largest financial institutions worldwide use it, along with over half of the top 25 P&C insurers and most major telecommunications and utility firms. Industry leaders in transportation, manufacturing, and technology have also been known to use Intelliscore as their primary risk indicating model.

In performance tests it has been found that 74% of accounts found to be risky were also in the lower 20% of the credit score range.

This means that Intelliscore's lowest credit scores did indeed account for almost 2/3 of the accounts that actually were risky.

Intelliscore now even has indicators that allow for different scoring depending on the business size. The new Intelliscore Plus has over 800 aggregates or factors that affect the credit scores. Scores are assessed on the more than 7.2 million businesses in Experian's database. And with Intelliscore, Plus Experian is using technology such as their BizSource and TrueSearch for increased data depth and better matching of business records.

Experian first takes a business and looks at data segments such as firmographics, public records, collections, and trade information, then places each business in one of three different models. The first is their Commercial Model, for small, medium, and larger businesses. Second is their Blended/ Owner Model, where the commercial data is then linked with the owner's information. Thirdly there is the Intelliscore Plus, or their percentile score. In segmenting business records this way, Experian can use more specific scoring for each individual business.

Intelliscore Plus, just like FICO, has multiple facets to the entire score makeup. The score is still based on the payment history of the business, but many other factors tie into percentages of the overall score. The Historical Behavior or payment history accounts for 5-10% of the total score. Current payment status, trade balances, and percent of accounts delinquent account for 50-60% of the score makeup.

The business' credit utilization affects 10-15% of the total score. This has to do with the amount of credit that has been extended to the business in relation to the balances they currently have on those accounts. The company profile, age of business, industry risk, and size of business assessed by number of employee's accounts for 5-10% of the total score. And 10-15% of the total score is determined based on the derogatory items, collections, liens, judgments, and bankruptcies that business has.

Model Weighting*	Business Aggregates
5-10%	Historical payment behavior, delinquency trends
50-60%	Current payment status - number / trade balance / percent of accounts delinquent
10-15%	Credit utilization
5-10%	Company profile- age of business, industry risk, employee size
10-15%	Derogatory items - collections, liens, judgments, bankruptcy

When Experian is assigning a business, a credit score they take many factors into account. They refer to these factors as predictive data and use this data to better determine a business's lending risk. Multiplr factors affect the score, including average balances on accounts, how recent are the delinquencies, what number and what percent of accounts are current versus delinquent, the percent of balances seriously delinquent, the overall utilization ratio, and any balances on leases.

Firmographis is what Experian refers to as the background information of a business. This factor considers the risks inherent in the business' specific industry and how many employees the business employs. Firmograhics also considers the length of time the business has been reporting to Experian. They have found that a business with a longer-standing Experian credit file is typically less at risk of defaulting. Inquiries are also considered with Firmographics.

Experian also provides consumer credit reports. They provide options for reports that reflect information about the business and the business owner called "blended" reports. They actually promote this as an added business, as studies have shown that consumer reports don't offer the most comprehensive assessment of risk on their own.

With blended reports Experian considers both factors from the business and from the consumer credit of the owner or personal guarantor. Factors considered are the number of accounts recently delinquent, number of derogatory payment accounts, number of accounts with 90% utilization, number of bankcards with 100% or more utilization, number of inquiries, and real estate inquiries.

Experian credit reports offer many details along with their scores, including business credit summaries and key facts about the business. Each report also provides business contact information, corporate registration details, and uniform commercial code filing data. Details relating to the business payment history are also included in the reports, including summaries of collections and payments, bankruptcy, judgment, and tax filings, even banking, insurance and leasing information.

Equifax

Equifax's main business credit scoring model is the Credit Risk Score. This score was created to enhance risk assessment throughout the account life cycle by predicting the probability of a new or existing small business customer becoming seriously delinquent on supplier accounts, or bankrupt, within a 12-month period.

Credit scores range from 1-100, with a lower score indicating a higher risk of serious delinquency. By definition the score predicts the likelihood of a business incurring a 90-days severe delinquency or charge-off over the next 12 months.

With Equifax, scores of 90 and above express that obligations are being paid as agreed. Scores from 80-89 indicate payments are being made 1-30 days overdue, while scores of 60-79 represent payments being paid 31-60 days past the agreed-upon due date. Credit scores ranging from 40-59 indicate payments being made 61-90 days overdue, while scores between 20-39 mean obligations are being paid 91-120 days overdue and scores between 1-19 mean obligations are being paid 120+ days past the due date.

Equifax also provides a business credit score for suppliers known as the Small Business Credit Risk Score for Suppliers. This model is designed to help credit grantors improve their risk assessment and reduce delinquency rates while helping to improve profitability. The score utilizes unique bank loans, lease information, credit card data, and supplier, Telco and utility credit history, public records and firmographic data from their own Equifax Commercial database.

The Small Business Credit Risk Score for Suppliers credit scores range from 101-816, with the lower score indicating a higher risk. If the business had a bankruptcy on file, they would have a 0 score. There are four major factors affecting the score.

These are how many years the business has been in business, whether there is evidence of judgments or liens, the length of time since the oldest financial account was open on the report, and whether the business has a 45% or higher trade utilization ratio.

Equifax also offers a Business Failure Risk Score with many reports. This Risk Score predicts the likelihood that the business will fail or file for bankruptcy within the next 12-month period. This model helps identify businesses that pose a greater risk for failure so that suppliers and credit grantors can take appropriate actions.

The Business Failure Risk Score considers information gathered from supplier trade information, firmographics, and public record information from Equifax's Commercial database. Business Failure Risk Scores range from 1000-1880, with a lower score indicating a higher risk. With this Risk Score a 0 indicates the business has filed a bankruptcy.

There are four reason codes indicating the top factors that affected the score. Unlike other risk scores, this unique score indicates the likelihood that the business will cease to exist within the next 12 months.

Equifax provides many details on each business for which it produces credit reports. Each report has a profile of the company with the business name, address, and phone numbers. Inquiries the business has made into other credit is also displayed, along with the business's credit score. Each report also lists the Risk Score and key factors affecting that score.

On the reports you can obtain for your own business Equifax provides a payment index explaining the credit score breakdown. There are even graphs that track your current utilization and the number of days you paid beyond the given terms.

Public records information is displayed, along with a credit report summary section including information on the number of accounts, how long credit has been active, number of charge-offs, total past due, most severe status within the last 24 months on any accounts, the single highest credit extended, the total current credit exposure, and the median and average open balances on accounts.

Equifax reports also show any recent credit activity for the business, financial information such as information on business cards, loans, and other credit extended by financial institutions. The reports also show the amount of credit usage and reflect any trending that Equifax has identified.

Equifax reports provide many details for each financial account listed on the business report. The account number and current account status is listed. A breakdown of the Equifax report status descriptions is available on the table above.

Each account also shows the date the account was last reported on and the date it was opened. It also lists the date the account was closed. All financial accounts listed on Equifax reports show the current credit limit for the account, the balance owed, and a full 24-month payment history is also available.

Equifax also reports details on non-financial accounts. These details include account number, account type, date reported, and date opened, date or last sale and the payment terms, the high credit and current credit limit, the account balance, past due amount, and aging categories if applicable. Public record accounts report the registered name, filing date, incorporation date, incorporation state, status, registry number, and contact name and address.

Each Equifax report has an additional information section with alternate company information, including DBA names, addresses, phone numbers, and the parent company if applicable. In this section they list guarantor information, comments from the business owners or credit grantors, and recent inquiries.

Building a Strong Business Foundation

The perception lenders, vendors, and creditors have of a business is critical to the business's ability to build strong business credit. Before applying for business credit, a business must insure it meets or exceeds all lender credibility standards. In total there are over 20 credibility standards that are necessary for a business to have a strong, credible foundation.

When building business credit, everything matters. Approval is sometimes based on the exact number of employees claimed on the application. In other cases, a business might be denied if they don't claim the right amount of vehicle gas usage in a month.

Certain types of phone numbers should not be used. While it is essential to ensure your number is listed in places the business credit reporting agencies and creditors will look,, if a business doesn't have the right type of phone number or if it isn't listed in the right places, the business will be denied credit.

The type of corporation you list, the years your company has been in business and the type of ownership all factor in to getting a business APPROVED for higher credit limits. Most importantly, knowing and understanding which of the thousands of creditors to apply to and in which order to apply are essentials in the business credit approval process.

The first step in building business credit is all about establishing credibility for the company. The business owner should think about the approval process from a lender's perspective to improve chances of approval. Lenders are in business to lend to companies they consider to be a "safe risk." They will be doing a number of underwriting checks to see if the business is "safe" enough for them to consider extending credit.

Part of establishing the business as a safe risk is following lenders' standards for approval. Complying helps the business establish credibility and is an important foundation for business credit building success.

Business Fundability is essential in getting approved for business credit. You won't find "Fundability" on Dictionary.com, so don't bother looking. Fundability is a phrase those of us in the lending industry have coined to describe how a business measures up in relation to the entire business lending and investing community.

Fundability is not just about business credit. It includes several components that determine how the overall business is seen by lenders, investors, insurers, suppliers, and more. Basically, the business was worth the risk for the business owner, but is it worth the risk for the lender? The answer will increasingly be "yes" as the business fundability grows.

By improving the fundability of the business, the business owner is truly improving the overall "health" of the business while greatly increasing the ability of the business to succeed now and in the future. The major components of Business Fundability include business bank accounts, business assets, business revenue, and the owners and their credit history.

Every lender has approval guidelines they follow when considering a loan application. Here are a few of the main items that typically get a business denied when trying to build business credit and obtain financing:

- no 411-directory assistance listing means no loan
- bank account balance rating of "low 5" likely means no loan
- having fewer than 5 trade credits accounts reporting to credit bureaus means no loan
- not having a credit file number will mean not getting that loan
- business credit scores below 70 usually mean no loan
- the lender may insist the business has a debt coverage ratio of 5:1 or better or deny the loan
- or a business might be turned away due to any of a host of other reasons

It only takes one reason for a lender to deny the application. And it is even tougher as many conventional banks offering funding require extensive documentation for a client to qualify. Some of this required documentation includes:

- interim financial statements
- most-recent Federal Tax Returns for each principal owner
- accountant-prepared financial statements including Profit & Loss statement and Balance Sheet for the last 3 years
- personal financial statements for each principal owner
- organization papers, such as incorporation papers, DBA papers, business licenses, etc.
- list of business and personal assets that can be used as collateral
- names and contact information for at least three credit references

These documents can be very difficult for a start-up business to supply, especially if they've never done any business before. Many banks expect a business to be already established before they request financing. But it is actually possible to get started without having an established business.

Building a Strong Foundation

One of the first aspects of an application a lender will look at is the business name. A business must use its exact business legal name. The full business name should include any recorded DBA filings the business is using. A business must also ensure the business name is exactly the same on the business corporation papers, all licenses, and bank statements.

Business credit can be built with almost any type of corporate entity. If the business owner truly wants to separate business credit from personal credit, their business must be a separate legal entity, not a sole proprietor or partnership.

Unless they have a separate business entity (Corporation or LLC) they might be "doing business" but they are not truly "a business". A business must be a Corporation or an LLC in order for business credit to be truly separate from personal credit.

Business credit cannot, and does not, exist for a sole proprietor. All that a sole proprietor has available are personal loans or lines of credit. This credit is tied to the business owner's personal social security number.

Every business entity must have a Federal Tax ID number (EIN) to apply for business credit, whether that business has employees or not. A Tax EIN number does for a business what your social security number does for you as a person. This number identifies the business to the Federal government and IRS.

The business Tax ID number is used to open business bank accounts and to build the business credit profile. A business owner must take the time to verify that all agencies, banks, and trade credit vendors have their business listed with the same tax ID number

A business must have a real brick-and-mortar building to look credible to most lenders. The address must be a real deliverable physical address. The business address cannot be a home address. The address cannot be a PO box or UPS address. Many lenders and merchants will not approve a business for credit unless this criterion is met.

There are a few popular solutions for business owners who might not have a real physical address. One of those solutions is an "Address Only" virtual office. With this type of office, a business can receive mail and packages at their own professional and real dedicated business address. That mail is then forwarded to wherever the business chooses.

Another business address solution is a "Virtual Office". With this type of office, the business has a real professional business address and a dedicated phone and fax number. This service commonly comes with receptionist services and sometimes also includes part-time use of fully furnished offices and meeting rooms.

A "True Office" is a real office a business owner can rent. The business will have its own full-time private office with receptionist services, dedicated phone and fax, Internet, full furnishings, meeting rooms, and many more amenities.

With any of these solutions a business can create the perception that it functions out of a big office, in many cases out of a major city. But in reality, it could just be a one-person home-based business. This boost in image credibility will help the business get approved for more credit and higher limits on the approved credit.

A business must also have a dedicated business phone number that is listed with 411 to appear credible to most merchants and lenders. The listing should be in directory assistance under the exact business name.

Lenders, vendors, creditors, and even insurance providers will verify that the business is listed with 411.

A toll-free number will give the business credibility, but the business must have a LOCAL business number for the listing with 411 directory assistance.

Lenders perceive 800 Number or toll-free phone numbers as a sign of business credibility. Even if the business owner is a single owner with a home-based business, a toll-free number provides the perception that the business is an even bigger company.

It's incredibly easy and inexpensive to set-up a virtual local phone number or a toll-free 800 number for any business. No business owner should ever use a cell or home phone number as their main business line. This can get that business "flagged" with the business credit reporting agencies as an un-established business that is too high a risk.

Lenders perceive a credible business as one with a fax number. Every business owner will need a fax number to receive important documents and to fax in credit applications to lenders and merchants. With e-faxes, which can be set up very affordably, you can have faxes be received and sent to you through email. And there are even some companies who can set up a company to send faxes over the internet from email.

Credit providers will research the company applying for credit on the Internet. It is best if they learned everything directly from that company's website. Not having a company website will severely hurt the chances of that business obtaining business credit. There are many places online that offer affordable business websites, so a business can have an Internet presence that displays an overview of the company's services and contact information.

Every business also needs a professional company email address. It's not only professional, but greatly helps the business' chances of getting approved for new credit. Setting up a business email address is too easy and inexpensive for a business owner to neglect.

When a business sets up its email addresses it's essential that they avoid using free email services like Yahoo and Hotmail. There is nothing worse than credit providers seeing an email address like rockout2012@gmail.com. The email address should be @company.com. A great example is an email like support@company.com or john.smith@company.com.

The business' banking history is vital to the business's future success of being able to secure larger business loans. The date the owner opened the business bank account is the day that many lenders consider the business to have become operational. So, if the business incorporated 10 years ago but the business bank account was just opened yesterday, then that business started yesterday. The longer the business banking history, the better the borrowing potential will be.

One of the most common mistakes when building credit for your company is non-matching business addresses on the business licenses. Even worse is not having the "required" licenses for your type of business to operate legally.

Every business owner needs to contact their State, County, and City Government offices to see if there are any licenses or permits required to operate their type of business. They must also ensure that state business filings are listed correctly, county license and/or permit filings are listed correctly, city license and/or permit filings are listed correctly, and IRS filings are listed correctly. They must also confirm that every agency, creditor, supplier, and trade credit vendor have their business listed the exact same way.

A business must be listed with the exact same spelling of the business name and the exact same address and phone number. For example, one might have you listed as "ABC, Inc.", while another has "AB Consultants", and yet another as "AB Consultants, Inc". There are also simple differences like those between "Suite 400", "# 400", and "Apt. 400".

The differences are important and should be corrected where possible. Every business owner should take the time to verify that main agencies (State, IRS, Bank, and 411 national directory) have their business listed the same way and with the Exact Legal Name. Also, they should take the time to ensure every bill (power bill, phone bill, landlord, etc.) has the business name listed correctly and comes to the business address.

All applicable business tax returns must have been filed for a business owner to have a credible foundation. There can't be any derogatory public records for the business including no liens, judgments, or lis pendens against the business. Many lenders will also want to see a business model when the business is applying for higher amounts of funding.

A business starts building a brand-new credit profile much the same way a consumer does. The business starts with no credit profile. The business gets approved for new credit that reports to the business credit reporting agencies.

The business uses the credit and pays the bill in a timely manner. As the business has established a positive business credit profile, and as the business continues using the credit and paying the bills on time, it will qualify for more credit.

The first step in business credit building is for the business owner to order a credit report for the business. It is very important for the business owner to know what really is being reported for that business in regard both to positive and derogatory information. The business owner will also want to actively monitor the business credit building and score building as it is taking place.

Business Credit Reports

Many business owners find, when they receive their Business Information Report from D&B, that they have a low PAYDEX score. They scratch their heads and wonder why their score is low even when they are paying the bills on time.

A business owner cannot find out which companies are reporting negative information to your file without having a credit report. But a business owner can obtain a list of all the companies that are reporting to the business credit file. Upon request, the business owner will get an alphabetical list of all the companies reporting to the business credit bureau as well as the number of times they reported.

To get the list a business owner can call a D&B representative and asked them for the list of companies reporting on their business. There must be at least five companies reporting before the representative will be able to pull this list.

On page 2 of the report will be an overview of the companies that have reported and the dollar-weighted payments. The Paydex score will also be on the report. Each of the companies listed will be sorted by supplier industry. If there are less than 20 companies on the list, the D&B representative might choose to simply read the list over the phone or e-mail the information to the business owner.

Other information on this report includes the total dollar amount of all trades reported, the largest amount that any one trade has reported, and the percentage of payments that have been made to the top ten (10) industries.

Business Credit reports are offered by Experian, Dun & Bradstreet, and Equifax. A business owner will first want to get a copy 4of their business credit reports to see what is being reported. They can visit http://www.smartbusinessreports.com/ for a copy of their Smart Business report. $49-99 is the current charge for a single report or credit monitoring

The Experian Smart Business credit report will tell the business owner how many trade lines are reporting and show if a business credit score has been assigned, if the business has an active Experian Business Profile, and if the business has had any recent credit inquires.

A Equifax Small Business Credit Report can be obtained here: http://www.equifax.com/small-business/credit-report/en_sb. It typically takes more time to create a file with Equifax Small Business than with D&B or Experian. This is why it's important for a business owner to apply with the credit providers who report to Equifax. Their reports currently run $99.95 for a full report.

Obtaining a Dun & Bradstreet number (D-U-N-S #) begins the process of building a business credit profile with Dun & Bradstreet. The D-U-N-S # will also play an important role in enabling the business to borrow without a personal guarantor. D&B's website is http://www.dnb.com/, and they are known to quote $299-$699 per DUNS Number with some type of package.

D&B also offers their DNBi SelfMonitor to monitor business credit during the building process. A subscription for D&B Self-Monitoring is $39-99 per month depending on the add-on options a business owner might choose.

Once a business sets up its credit report and pays some bills on time it should have a high PAYDEX score. It is then vital that the business maintains its report.

The business owner should check the business report periodically. They may want to consider purchasing the Monitoring Service that D&B offers. This service allows a business to receive alerts when new positive or negative information appears on the report. There are several areas that a business owner will be notified of if they change including:

- Credit Rating
- Suits, liens or business judgments
- PAYDEX score changes
- Changes to financial statements
- Other significant business news

Nearly every D&B report contains some errors, so a business owner shouldn't be alarmed to review their business report and find an error or two. Most problems needing resolution will be dealt with through the eUpdate website; however, any major issues will need special attention. In those cases, it's best to pay D&B to get an account representative to fix the problem quickly and efficiently so that it doesn't affect the business file.

It is extremely important that the business credit file remain accurate. The Fair Credit Reporting Act does not apply to businesses as it does with consumer reports. If there is something wrong on the business credit report, or if a step is skipped in setting it up, there is no legal recourse to have that information removed. If the file was set up incorrectly, there's a good chance the business credit file could be put in the “High Risk” category, making it nearly impossible to remove inaccuracies.

A business credit report can be started in much the same way as a consumer report commonly is, with small credit cards. The business can be approved for small credit cards to help it build an initial credit profile. These types of initial cards in the business world are commonly referred to as "vendor credit".

A vendor line of credit is when a company (vendor) extends a line of credit to a business on "Net 15, 30, 60 or 90" day terms. This means that the business can purchase their products or services up to a maximum dollar amount and the business owner has 15, 30, 60 or 90 days to pay the bill in full.

So, if the business owner is set up on Net 30 terms and were to purchase $300 worth of goods today, then that $300 is due within the next 30 days. With vendor accounts business owners can get products and services for their business needs and defer the payment on those for 15 days or more, thereby easing cash flow.

And some vendors will approve the company for Net 30 payment terms upon verification of as little as an EIN number and a 411 listing. It is important that business owners always apply first without using their SSN. Some vendors will request it, and some will even say on the phone they need to have it, but it is best to submit first without it.

One of the main reasons that 90% of business owners don't have access to business credit is that they don't know where to go to get VENDOR accounts to build their business credit profiles and scores. Vendors are the Gate Keepers of business credit. They are the REAL secret of business credit building.

A business owner can go to Home Depot today and apply for business credit. But they would typically be denied or approved only with a personal guarantee. To get approved with them with NO personal guarantee, their business must first meet the business credit qualifying requirements. The problem is most people never know what their qualifying criteria are. So, they apply and are approved only with a personal guarantee or are denied all together.

A business owner can't just walk into a merchant like Wal-Mart, Staples, or Home Depot and get approved for business credit with no guarantee. They first must have a good business credit score and 5 or more trade-lines reporting on your business credit to get approved.

Here is where most people get stuck. They can't get credit since they have no credit, so they are never able to build their business credit. The real secret to business credit is Vendor accounts. With these accounts a business owner can get approved for credit with vendors who will report to the business reporting agencies. This makes it easy for a business owner to build 5 or more trades and establish an excellent score.

A business will need to start with "preferred vendors." These are vendors who are known to extend credit to all businesses, even those with no credit history. Remember, we said from the very beginning that it takes 90 to 120 days to build business credit scores. The credit reporting cycles are the main reason for that, and it cannot be done faster.

When the first Net 30 account reports as "tradelines" to Dun & Bradstreet, the DUNS system will automatically activate the business credit file if it isn't already. This is also true for Experian and Equifax.

A business will need at least five (5) vendor accounts reporting on the credit to truly be established. If these accounts are paid promptly an excellent business credit score will also be established. With these new accounts and score a business will be able to start getting approved for revolving credit accounts.

It is important for a business owner to know that some vendors require an initial prepaid order before they can approve a business for terms. It is also essential that every established vendor account is being used and paid promptly in full, as required.

Business credit building is much faster than consumer credit building. Still, it does take some time and a business owner must be patient and allow time for the vendors' reporting cycles to get into the reporting systems. It typically takes 3 cycles of "Net" accounts reporting to build credit scores initially.

This means it could take as long as 90 days between the initial payment to the merchant and the account report on the business credit report. It does typically happen faster, within 30-60 days, but it can take as long as 90 days or 3 reporting cycles.

Once the accounts are reported a credit history has begun. The business will then have a business credit score based on how the bills were paid, on time, early, or late. As more and more accounts are added to the credit report more trade lines are established and the "deeper" the credit profile becomes.

Merchants who offer higher limits and revolving credit cards will want to see "deep" credit profiles. This means they will want to see a business credit report that has many trade lines that are being paid as agreed or early each month.

To get approved for more accounts the business will also want to have reporting trades with higher credit limits. Many merchants who offer revolving credit cards will want to see a business credit profile that has a lot of trade lines, and some of those trades should have higher limits of $10,000 or more. As the business has more accounts reporting as paid-as-agreed, other vendor sources will approve the business for higher credit limit accounts.

Vendor sources are not easy to locate. This is one of the main reasons very few businesses have established business credit. Most business owners look but can't find reliable sources who will offer them the initial vendor credit they need to start building a business credit profile.

Once a business owner locates some vendor sources the other main challenge, they will face is the knowledge and understanding of what it takes to get approved with each source. Most merchants who offer vendor credit don't promote that they do so, and they certainly don't make their underwriting guidelines public.

So, if the business owner does find some vendor sources, the next challenge is for them to know enough about the underwriting guidelines to be approved. This causes frustration, as many businesses apply for initial credit to build their credit profile but are denied for reasons unknown.

In the business world lenders and merchants do not need to disclose why they deny an application. This is unlike the consumer industry, where this information has to be provided to the consumer, even including the credit bureaus that were pulled to make the denial decision.

In the business world a business can be denied for credit and never notified at all. Lenders can also have no requirement to provide the business with any details as to why they were denied.

This has always been one of the biggest challenges with building business credit. Owners don't know where to apply, what the guidelines are, and when they apply and are denied they are rarely provided any details allowing them to correct their issues and reapply to get approved.

In this book I will provide many sources that can be used to build vendor credit. These sources are like gold when it comes to business credit building: they are the secret to getting approved for the initial trade lines to start building business credit, establishing a positive business credit score, and starting to get approved for revolving credit card sources.

Starter Vendor Credit Sources

One vendor who is great for business credit building is Radio Shack, one of the nation's most experienced and trusted consumer electronics specialty retailers. They also are a great vendor to use when building credit. Radio Shack offers products most business owners will need and want, like computers, phones, batteries, cables and connectors and much more.

There is a lot of funding available that will start the reporting process for the business and place the business on all other lenders' radars. Radio Shack is one of those creditors who reports to D&B and Experian. They will pull a business credit report to see how the business had paid bills in the past. If there isn't enough data on the business credit report, they will ask for bank and trade references

To be approved most business will need to have been in business for at least 2 years. A D&B number is required, and credit references will be required as well. Like most vendors, Radio Shack offers payment terms of Net 30 for their vendor accounts. Currently you can call 1-800-442-7221 to get an application. Fill it out and fax back it back to 817-415-3909

Quill is another very popular vendor account. Quill's vendor account provides payment terms of Net 30. Quill sells office supplies, cleaning supplies, packing and shipping supplies, school supplies, printing supplies, and more. From filing and storage to hand-held computers, Quill has a wide range of discounted top-name brand products.

Quill reports to D&B. Typically, they require that a business place its first order before being considered for a Net 30 account. If the business has a D&B score established, it will probably get approved with the initial order.

For new businesses with little to no credit history, the business will probably be put on a 90-day prepayment schedule. If an order is made every month for 90 days, they will more than likely approve a Net 30 account. New businesses can start out with smaller limits that will increase when bills are paid on time every month.

Laughlin Associates will make sure your business is in corporate compliance with all documents, including Articles of Incorporation, Corporate Minutes, Corporate Resolutions, List of Officers, and more.

Laughlin Associates will approve any business that is listed in 411 and has a business bank account and EIN number. They will report all payments to Experian. It takes 30-60 days for the first trade line to show up on the credit report from the date of purchase. Laughlin Associates also offers low monthly payments and they report as a Net 30 account.

Monopolize Your Marketplace is a little-know company that is a great source for building business credit. They are a great starting vendor as they will approve most businesses for vendor credit. They report accounts to Experian and offer net 30 terms.

Monopolize Your Marketplace offers a marketing system that teaches businesses about how to market their business. They provide 10 audio CDs and over 11 hours of materials. The CDs focus on topics including the marketing equation, MYM technology, industry category strategies, the master marketing letter, and more.

This account is a perfect way to start building business credit. They will approve most businesses for at least $400 in credit. They offer a payment plan for their system, which is 4 payments of $59.99. They will then report those payments to Experian. To be approved the business will need an EIN number, a real deliverable address, and an open business bank account.

ITC Web Services is another great starter vendor source. ITC reports to all three business credit reporting agencies Dun & Bradstreet, Experian, and Equifax. They offer a great vendor account with 30-day net terms.

ITC offers many web and technical services including website creation. They offer affordable websites and will even revamp a business's current website. They provide Joomla, Drupal, PHP, and MySQL website development.

They also help businesses establish professional email addresses, web applications, flash animation design, logo design, computer support, web banner design, and mobile device app development.

ITC Web Services will approve a business for a vendor account with no personal credit check required from the business owner, and no personal guarantee required. The business must be listed in 411 to be approved and have a business bank account open and an EIN number.

Business Marketing Services is another company that offers a starter vendor credit account. This account reports to Experian and Dun & Bradstreet, and it will be offered on net 30 terms. They offer custom website creation, social media marketing, search engine optimization, logo creation, and more.

To be approved a business must provide proof of a valid operation U.S. business. They will typically require 30% payment upfront on purchases but will extend credit to almost all businesses for the other 70% of the purchase paid over a 5-month period.

Market Click Internet Marketing is another little-known source offering a powerful starter vendor account. Market Click offers online services including search engine optimization, setting up websites for maximum online exposure, and more. They offer net 30 terms and report to Dun & Bradstreet only.

Most businesses will be approved without requiring any personal guarantee from the business owner. They also rarely require a personal credit check. It will take them about 30-60 days to first report the trade line to Dun & Bradstreet.

A Printer 4 U offers most businesses, even startup businesses, a credit line of up to $2,500. They offer graphic and logo design services, printing, banner creation, and much more.

They report to Experian and Dun & Bradstreet and offer net 30 terms. They will typically require a 50% upfront payment on all orders; the business can then finance the rest.

A Printer 4 U will require the business phone number to be listed with 411. They will also require the business address, phone number, bank account information, and trade references for approval. They require no personal guarantee and will approve businesses with no personal credit check required from the business owner.

Another great starter vendor account is offered through Paramount Payment Systems. Paramount gives businesses the ability to offer payment terms to customers on products and services they currently offer.

They will accept customer checks, front the business the money from that check, then charge a fee to the customer to collect on those checks. They give the business owner the funds right away, and there is no recourse for the business owner if their customers' check doesn't clear.

Paramount offers net 30 terms and reports directly to Dun & Bradstreet. They don't work with some industries such as web design, jewelers, used cars, some basic retail stores, and online businesses. A business must provide an EIN to be approved, show how long they have been in business, and 2 years of credit references.

Other Vendor Credit Sources

The aforementioned accounts are perfect starter accounts for business credit building. They are great accounts because they work for most businesses, even brand-new startup businesses. There are still a lot of other available vendor accounts. Many others come from very well-known companies. But some of these require that a business be in business longer or have other established trade lines to qualify.

Staples is one of these companies that offers vendor accounts for already established businesses. Staples is a mega-retailer that sells office supplies, among other business services. They offer a net 30 reporting business credit trade line that reports to all three business credit reporting agencies, Dun & Bradstreet, Experian, and Equifax.

Staples will check with Experian, Equifax, and Dun & Bradstreet to see if the business already has a credit history. The amount of money they approve a business for depends on the already-established credit history the business has. If the business has no or little credit history, the business owner will typically be asked for a personal credit check and personal guarantee. They will also check to ensure the business is listed in 411 and has an EIN number.

ULine Shipping Supplies is one of the leading distributers of shipping, industrial, packing materials, even janitorial products. They offer a vendor account that can be used for business credit building. This account is offered on net 30 terms and reports to Dun & Bradstreet.

ULine requires every business to have a DUNS number established with Dun & Bradstreet before they can be approved. They will look at the business credit report, searching for existing trade lines, and they might also require trade and bank references. They typically want to see at least 2 trade references and 1 bank reference.

If they pull a business credit report and see little to no credit history, they will typically require a few orders be pre-paid first before offering their net 30 account. They might also ask for financials before approving a business if it has little to no business credit history established.

Home Depot is one of the world's largest retailers for home and building supplies. They offer a vendor business credit account on net 30 terms that reports to Experian and Dun & Bradstreet.

For a business to be approved, the business must have been in business for at least 3 years. If the business has been open 3 years or longer, they typically won't ask for a personal guarantee from the business owner or require a personal credit check. If the business has been open less than 3 years than they will require a personal credit check and guarantee from the business owner. They require an EIN number from the business for approval.

Grainger Industrial Supply is a popular, well-known source that thousands of suppliers use for electrical fasteners, fleet maintenance HVACR hardware, janitorial, material handling, pneumatics, power tools, pumps, and more. They offer a net 30 account that is reported to Dun & Bradstreet quarterly.

If the business has a business license, they will typically be approved for $1,000 account or less. If the business has trade and bank references, it will typically be approved for accounts over $1,000. They will require the business provide an EIN number.

Labor Ready is a leading multinational source of dependable labor for companies across many industries. They offer a vendor account on net 7-day terms that reports to Dun & Bradstreet. They require a valid tax ID number to approve a business. They will approve a business for this net 7-day account with no personal credit check or personal guarantee required from the business owner.

Sherwin Williams offers a net 20-day vendor account that reports to Dun & Bradstreet. They offer a wide variety of products ranging from coatings for plastics, metal and wood serving many industries. They will pull both personal and business credit for approval, and will typically approve a business with an established, strong credit profile with Dun & Bradstreet.

Macys is a large department store that can help businesses with many needs including employee recognition programs, dress code programs, and special holiday and thank-you gifts. Their vendor account is offered on net 30 terms and reports to Dun & Bradstreet.

Macys will only approve a business for their vendor account if the business already has a positive Dun & Bradstreet credit score established. They will compare the business score against the industry average score to determine approval. They require no personal credit check or personal guarantee from the business owner. They commonly request bank references for approval also.

Budget Car Rentals offers another good vendor account for business credit building. Their account reports to Equifax and Dun & Bradstreet and is approved as a net 30-day terms. A business must already have had a Budge Express Account for at least 2 years and spent over $5,000. For approval the business must also be listed in 411 and have at least 20 employees.

For the best business credit-building success a business should obtain at least five revolving business credit card accounts along with the five vendor accounts. These accounts report to the business credit agencies in different ways and carry more weight than the vendor credit that was used to initially start building the business credit.

After five tradelines have been established and reported, the business will be able to start getting approved for revolving business credit accounts. A revolving credit account is one that allows the business to pay a "minimum due" per month and not the full outstanding balance. These accounts normally report to Experian, D&B and sometimes Equifax. Because of how they report, these accounts will help build business credit on a larger scale than just the Net 30-day vendors alone

Most merchants and major retailers offer business credit, they just don't advertise it. There is no benefit to the merchant to promote credit with no personal liability if the business owner is willing to take on that liability. So, they don't promote their business credit cards and regularly ask for an SSN.

Staples is one example that we met in the previous chapter. They will verify 411 directories while the business owner is on hold. They will check that the business credit files are open with D&B and Experian. They also check to see if the business name and address matches the 411 listing. They offer revolving payment terms.

Dell is another popular revolving business credit account. Business owners visit Dell to buy computers and accessories for your home or business. The Dell Business Credit Account is a revolving line of credit that provides an easy way to finance purchases of Dell equipment.

Dell reports to D&B. They regularly approve for accounts with limits up to $10,000 as long as the business owner has a D&B Paydex score of 75 or higher. They require that a business have been open for 6 months before they will approve that business. They will sometimes check personal credit during their approval process. Dell offers revolving payment terms.

Lowe's is another popular revolving business credit account. Lowe's offers a huge selection of tools, kitchen appliances, cabinets, cabinet hardware, countertops and paint, and much more. Customers can purchase online or at their local Lowe's center. Lowe's offers a fast, online approval and revolving business credit accounts.

Lowe's reports to D&B and Experian. Applicants can apply online for approval with a D&B number generated businesses are typically approved for credit limits of $1,000-5,000.

Businesses that have been open less than 3 years will require a personal guarantor unless a good D&B and/or Experian score is established.

Once a business owner has obtained a total of 10 reported accounts including vendor and revolving accounts, it can then start qualifying for real credit cards through Visa and MasterCard. Of the ten open accounts at least one account should have a high credit limit of $10,000 or more to qualify for Visa and MasterCard credit.

Most major merchants offer business credit that businesses can apply for. Many of these accounts offer credit limits of $10,000+. A business can get multiple Visa, MasterCard and AMEX cards and continue increasing limits.

Within a few months of starting the business credit building process, the business will qualify for thousands in real useable credit. Within 6-12 months the business will have access to over $50,000 in revolving credit with major retailers. In 1-2 years, the business can then continue on to qualify for $100,000-$250,000, depending on how it utilizes its newly acquired credit.

A business can also secure $50-150,000 credit lines on the basis of business credit with limited income document requirements. $250,000 credit lines are available with full income verification. Most of these credit lines come with check-writing capability and a linked debit card.

Starter Store Online Credit Source

There are many merchants who offer revolving credit accounts for businesses. Some of these accounts are starter accounts which work great to help a business first start building their business credit. These accounts will usually work for newer businesses with only a few vendor accounts reporting as trade lines on the business credit.

Staples, the office products mega-retailer, offers a great revolving account on top of the vendor account mentioned in the previous chapter. This account reports to Experian and Dun & Bradstreet and is a revolving account, not a net 30 account.

To approve a business for the revolving account they require the business be listed with 411 and have an EIN number. Staples will check to see if the business has credit profiles open with Experian and Dun & Bradstreet.

They will also check to ensure the business address and phone number matches the 411 listing. With prior business credit established they will not require a personal guarantee from the business owner. If no business credit is present with Experian or Dun & Bradstreet, Staples will do a credit check on the business owner and will require a personal guarantee.

Office Depot is another office product mega-retailer that provides office products, office supplies, office furniture, and more. They also provide a good, starter, revolving business credit account. Their revolving account reports to both Experian and Dun & Bradstreet.

Office Depot will check the business' credit profile with Experian or Dun & Bradstreet before approval. If one business credit reporting agencies has no or little information reporting, they will check the other source. If the business has little to no credit a personal guarantee from the business owner will be required.

Even with a personal guarantee provided, this account will report on the business credit reports, not the personal credit reports. The approval amount will be dependent on the business credit scores they pull. They might also request trade references if there is no business credit score or limited credit reporting.

There are many other accounts that are available for business credit building that are revolving accounts. These accounts might have more stringent requirements for approval than basic starter accounts have.

Wal-Mart is one of the best-known retailers in the world. They offer a massive assortment of products, including electronics, toys, home, garden, baby products, and much more. Their account is revolving and reports to both Experian and Equifax.

A business should be approved for this account if it has some business credit already established with Equifax and Dun & Bradstreet. They will also require a business credit score of 75 or higher, reflecting that the business pays its obligations as agreed each month. If the business can't get approved due to limited credit, they will still offer approval with a personal guarantee from the business owner.

Costco Wholesale is an international chain of membership warehouses. They offer an American Express business account with revolving terms that reports to Dun & Bradstreet.

They will look at the business credit of the business and the personal credit of the business owner with all three credit reporting agencies. They also require the business has an EIN number and they will require a personal guarantee from the business owner for any business open less than 2 years.

Amazon.com is an online shopping company that provides books, magazines, music, videos, electronics, computers, software, apparel and accessories, and much more. They report to Experian, Equifax, and Dun & Bradstreet and offer a revolving business credit account.

They offer their revolving account with no personal guarantee so long as the business has an EIN number and has been open at least 3 years. Amazon issues credit limits ranging from $500- 2,500, depending on the amount of business credit the business already has established.

Dell offers one of the most well-known accounts for business credit building. Dell sells computers, accessories, and other computer systems for small to large businesses. This is an account most companies who offer business credit know about, and commonly recommend. Dell offers a revolving account that reports to Dun & Bradstreet.

Dell commonly approves businesses for over $10,000 in credit as long as the business has and established business credit profile and score about 75 reflecting many accounts that have been paid-as-agreed. They require a business to be open for at least 6 months to approve the business with no credit check or guarantee required from the business owner.

Lowes offers tools, kitchen appliances, cabinets, countertops, paints, and much more relating to home improvement. They also offer a revolving business credit account that reports to Experian and Dun & Bradstreet.

They will typically approve a business for $1,000 or more in credit. They will look at the already established business credit profile with Dun & Bradstreet. If the Paydex credit score is over 85, they will typically approve the business for credit of $5,000 or more.

Lowes will approve a business for business credit with no personal credit check or guarantee from the business owner so long as the business has been open for over 3 years. If the business has a strong business credit profile and score, they might also approve the business with no personal guarantee required.

Sears offers a large abundance of products including appliances, lawn tractors, tools, and much more. Their business credit account reports to all three business credit reporting agencies, Dun & Bradstreet, Experian, and Equifax.

They require good business credit scores for approval and will look at the business scores from Dun & Bradstreet. If there are no scores with D&B, they will then check credit scores with Experian and Equifax business.

They will not require a personal guarantee from the business owner with a strong business credit score established. To be approved with no personal guarantee a business must be open at least 2 years. The business must also have an EIN number for business credit approval.

There are many sources available for business credit gas cards. These accounts are offered through many of the major fuel companies around the country. These accounts are great for business owners to use for fuel and other convenience store purchases. These accounts are especially good for truck drivers and other businesses that have vehicles on the road as part of their business model.

BP offers a business credit card that reports to Dun & Bradstreet and is a revolving credit account. This card can be used are more than 12,500 BP stations around the globe. This account can be used for a business fleet's fuel and maintenance needs anywhere MasterCard is accepted.

To be approved a business will need to show its tax ID number. BP will look at Experian, Dun & Bradstreet, and Equifax scores. If the business has strong credit profiles and scores, the business can then be approved with no personal guarantee from the business owner as long as the business has been open 3 years or longer.

Chevron also offers a great business gas card that is revolving and reports to Dun & Bradstreet. This account can be used at both Chevron and Texaco stations and can be used for gasoline, tires, batteries, and more.

A business will need at least a 75 Paydex credit score with Dun & Bradstreet and must have been in business at least 18 months to be approved with no personal credit check or guarantee required from the business owner.

Speedway Super America also offers a great business credit gas card that reports to Experian and Dun & Bradstreet and is revolving. To be approved the business must have been in business for at least 1 year.

Sinclair Oil also offers a gas merchant account. It is a revolving account that reports to Dun & Bradstreet. The account can only be used at Sinclair stations. No personal guarantee or credit check is required with established business credit history and positive scores.

CSI offers a corporate fleet MasterCard account that is accepted at nearly every retail and diesel CSI fueling location in the U.S. This card is accepted at over 180,000 stations nationwide. This account is revolving and is reported to Experian and Equifax.

CSI requires that 10 accounts be reported on the business credit reports before they will approve a business for a revolving business credit account. They also require that one of the trade lines have a high credit limit of $10,000 or higher before they will approve that business for credit.

They will require the business has an EIN number and includes a copy of a voided check, copy of a utility bill, the business address, business phone number, and they will want to see all required business licenses.

Other Merchant Credit Sources

Sam's Club offers a revolving business credit account that reports to Experian and Dun & Bradstreet. Sam's Club is a warehouse retail chain that offers office supplies, business furniture, vending items, cleaning supplies, paper products, food service supplies, computers and more.

Sam's requires that 10 accounts be reported on the business credit reports before they will approve a business for a revolving business credit account. They will require the business has an EIN number and includes a copy of a voided check, copy of a utility bill, the business address, business phone number, and they will want to see all required business licenses.

Key Bank offers a MasterCard that can be used anywhere that accepts MasterCard. With this account a business can earn points that can be redeemed for airline travel, merchandise, gift certificates, and more. They offer a 0% introductory rate for the first 6 six months. This revolving account reports to Experian, Equifax, and TansUnion.

Key Bank requires that the business credit report have 10 reporting trade lines before they will approve that business. They also require that one of the trade lines have a high credit limit of $10,000 or higher before they will approve that business for credit. They will request a personal credit check and guarantee from the business owner if the business doesn't match these conditions.

They will require the business has an EIN number and includes a copy of a voided check, copy of a utility bill, the business address, business phone number, and they will want to see all required business licenses.

There is a Volvo MasterCard that is offered through Wright Express that is a great revolving business credit account. This account reports to both Experian, and Equifax. They require that the Dun & Bradstreet business credit report have ten reporting trade lines before they will approve that business. They also require that one of the trade lines have a high credit limit of $10,000 or higher before they will approve that business for credit.

They will require financials to approve a business with no credit check or personal guarantee required from the business owner. They will also require that the business has an EIN number and includes a copy of a voided check, copy of a utility bill, the business address, business phone number, and they will want to see all required business licenses.

If a business uses cars, vans, or trucks, the Fleet One Local Fuel Card is a great business credit solution. This account is offered on net 14-day terms, and reports to all three business credit reporting agencies, Dun & Bradstreet, Experian, and Equifax. This card can be used for vehicle fuel and maintenance.

The Fleet- One Local Fleet Card requires that the business credit report have 10 reporting trade lines before they will approve that business. They also require that one of the trade lines have a high credit limit of $10,000 or higher before they will approve that business for credit. They will request a personal credit check and guarantee from the business owner if the business doesn't have 10 trade lines with at least one with a $10,000 high credit limit.

They will require the business has an EIN number and includes a copy of a voided check, copy of a utility bill, the business address, business phone number, and they will want to see all required business licenses.

Bank Rates

It is essential that a business owner separate their personal and business bank accounts. This is critical in running a successful business. One of the major financial tools used to accomplish this is a business bank account. A business bank account helps maintain accurate records, prepare reports, make deposits, withdrawals, wire transfers, issue checks, and much more.

Whether a business owner decides to open an account at a national, regional, or local bank, credit union, or community bank, they should select a bank that can best cater to the needs of their business. While every bank offers various types of financial business products, each serving a specific need, one thing remains the same throughout: bank credit.

Bank credit is the total amount of borrowing capacity a business can obtain from the banking system. This is not the same as business credit, which is a much broader category of lenders such as suppliers, credit card issuers, or leasing companies.

A business can secure more business credit quickly as long as it has a minimum of one bank reference and an average daily account balance of at least $10,000 for the past three months. This yields a "Bank Rating" of Low-5 (meaning an ADB of $5,000 to $30,000). A lower rating, say a High-4, or balance of $7,000 to $9,999 won't put a stop to the business's application, but it will slow down the approval process.

This rating is the average minimum balance maintained in the business bank account over a three (3) month period. A $10,000 balance will rate as "Low 5″, $5,000 rates as "Mid 4″, $999 rates as "High 3″, and so on. The main goal should be to maintain a minimum "Low 5" bank rating ($10,000) for at least 3 months. Unfortunately, without at least a "low 5″ rating, most banks will assume the business has little ability to repay a loan or a line of credit.

Business owners should do whatever they can to keep at least $10,000 in their account over a 90-day period. The money should be kept there just to ensure the bank rating is high enough to increase future financing approvals. Each cycle is based on the balance rating during the previous three-month period. So, before a business decides to apply for credit, it should keep a balance rating of "low 5" for the past three months.

It is also essential that the business owner ensures that their business bank accounts are reported exactly the way all their business records are, with the exact same physical address (no P.O. Box) and phone number.

It is vitally important that every credit agency and trade credit vendor, every record-keeper (financial records, income tax, web addresses and e-mail addresses, directory assistance), also lists the business name and address the same way. No lender is going to stop to consider all the ways a business might be listed, when they look into the business' "credit-worthiness". If they can't find what they need easily they will simply deny the application.

It is essential that a business manages its bank account responsibly. This means the business should avoid writing non-sufficient funds (NSF) checks at all costs as it destroys bank ratings. Non-sufficient-funds checks are something no business can let happen. It's even a good idea for the business to add overdraft protection to their bank account as soon as possible to avoid NSFs.

It is also very important that a business show a positive cash flow. The cash coming in and going out of a company's bank account should reflect a positive free cash flow. Positive free cash flow is the amount of revenue left over after the company has paid all its expenses. When the account shows a positive cash flow it indicates that the business is generating more revenue than is used to run the company. It's important to also recognize that banks are motivated to lend to a business that has consistent deposits.

A business owner must also make regular deposits to maintain a positive bank rating. Consistent deposits coming into the business bank account are looked upon very favorably. So, it is vital that a business owner make a lot of consistent deposits, more than the withdrawals they are making.

Bank credit is not only based on monthly deposits, balance rating, and check history, but also includes the age of the account, the bank products the business uses, and any savings account or investments the business has.

A seasoned bank account shows stability and longevity in the eyes of lenders. Keeping a healthy and long-standing relationship with a bank is also crucial for all companies. A good, stable, relationship with a bank that reflect longevity will be highly appreciated by lenders considering lending that business money.

Beyond just the bank rating, a business' bank should also act as a trusted advisor that can assist in growing the business.

It helps a business to consider working with a financial institution that specializes in providing banking services tailored to their specific industry.

Working with a lender that already understands their business makes it much easier to get a loan approved, compared with other lenders. This is because most lenders have difficulty assessing the credit risk of most small businesses or some any industries they know little about.

While profit and loss statements, tax returns, business credit and personal credit checks are common requirements in the lending process, it is much easier for a lender to underwrite the business' financial risk when it truly understands and specializes in making loans to a company in an industry, they are familiar and comfortable with.

The main reason most business owners build their business credit is to gain access to revolving credit accounts and cash funding. There are many sources that will give businesses funding based on their business credit. Those sources offer an abundance of different funding options to help businesses meet their ever-changing needs.

Most business owners tend to rely on their bank when funding is needed. The problem with this is that banks only have access to limited financing options. And most financing options banks do offer look at all the business financials, the personal credit and assets of the owner, and other business factors such as revenue and assets.

These loans, such as SBA insured loans, are tough to qualify for, as all aspects of the business must be perfect to be approved. This is why it is essential that a business owner work with a company who can offer many financing options through many lending institutions and investors, not just the limited sources banks offer.

Many types of available financing will not look at all the business financials, or the assets or credit of the owner, or even the revenue and business assets. There are many sources of financing available that only focus on certain aspects of the business, not the entire business itself.

For example, Purchase Order financing is a way to secure money for a business quickly. With this option a factoring company is only focusing on outstanding purchase orders, and nothing else. The lender is more concerned with the business client's ability to pay than the business itself, and the lender will even collect on the outstanding purchase orders for the business.

The business owner's personal credit and assets don't really tie into the lending approval decision; they are mainly concerned with only the business's purchase orders.

Account Receivable financing focuses on receivables, Equipment Financing focuses on what equipment the business owns, Revenue Financing focuses only on the business revenue. These are only a few of many business financing options that are available which focus only on certain aspects of the business, not the entire business.

This makes it easy for a business owner to obtain financing based on the strengths of their business, while ensuring lenders ignore the weaknesses.

Another benefit of having finance options is that monthly payments can also vary. With an SBA loan, payments are set on how much the business must repay each month. So, if that business has a slow month, it might be tough to repay that loan payment. But many finance options limit how much a business must pay back depending on how much revenue they are bringing in.

For example, $50,000 can be obtained through a Merchant Advance and the business will be charged a small percentage on future credit card sales until it pays back the loan. If the credit card sales drop in a month, so does the loan payment. So as sales fluctuate so does the loan payment.

Business Revenue lending works the same as it is based on business revenue. If monthly revenue drops in a month, so does the loan payment.

4 "C" s of Business Lending

In lending when we look to see if a client is fundable, we are looking for one of the 4 "C" s. A business owner doesn't need all of the 4 Cs, only 1 to secure funding.

The first C is Cash Flow. When an existing business has good cash flow it can qualify for business funding. If the business has verifiable cash flow this substantially increases the chances of that business being approved for funding. There are many funding programs the business might qualify for including Business Revenue Lending.

If the business doesn't have cash flow it still might have Collateral, the second C. Collateral for a business is really the business assets. Many things can be used as collateral including equipment, purchase orders, even account receivables. Having Collateral greatly increases the chances of a business being approved for funding.

If a business doesn't have cash flow or collateral it can still qualify for business funding. Lenders also look at your business Credit to qualify a business. Business Credit is the third C. Lenders will lend money with no personal guarantee based on the business credit profile and score. If the business has a good business credit profile it can use that as security to obtain funding.

If you don't have business credit built now, call me so I can help you quickly build an excellent business credit score and profile.

Maybe your business is just starting, and it doesn't yet have business credit, cash flow, or collateral. You can still qualify for funding. Lenders will then use your personal credit to qualify the business for funding. Personal Credit is the fourth and final C that lenders will look at when deciding whether to approve a business for funding.

Credit lines up to $250,000 are available today even for startup businesses with personal credit scores as low as a 650 FICO. These types of unsecured credit lines do not look at revenue or financials. The business owner's personal credit is all that is used to qualify for funding. All a business owner needs are 1 of the 4 "C" s to qualify for business funding.

Secured vs. Unsecured Funding

Secured funding is easier to be approved for. Even if the business owner has credit issues, you can still obtain many types of secured funding. This is because secured funding is using something as collateral for the funding they are receiving.

When you own a business there are many business assets that can use as collateral to obtain funding. Equipment financing for example leverages equipment as collateral for the debt. Purchase order financing uses purchase orders as collateral, while account receivable factoring uses receivables as collateral.

Real estate can be used as collateral and so can revenue. And since these financing options are using an element of the business as security, personal or business credit doesn't have to be great to qualify.

With good credit, a score of 650 or higher, then a business owner should qualify for unsecured funding options also. Unsecured funding is where the bank will lend money or approve for a credit line with no security required.

This means the business owner will not need to leverage any aspect of their business as collateral. The lender will base the lending decision on the quality of the personal or business credit profile. Either your personal or business credit profiles can be used to get approved.

With even a 650 personal credit score or higher, a business can qualify for these kinds of unsecured funding options. And with a good business credit profile built a business can also qualify for large amounts of business funding.

Interest rates on unsecured debts are obviously higher than secured debts, as the lender's risk is higher. Still, a business owner can obtain good working capital loans and credit lines at very reasonable interest rates and payments.

Secure Money Before It's Needed

In lending most applications are denied when the applicant needs money the most. Lenders lend based on risk. And the better a business is doing, the lower the risk it is from a lender's prospective. Still most business owners don't look for money until they actively, and sometimes desperately, need it.

Maybe it is an AC unit going out or freezer breaking, but something usually happens that costs much more than what is on hand. This is not the time that most business owners want to be looking for money. Instead, even major problems can be fixed without even a little hiccup if money is sitting and waiting.

This is one of many reasons business owners should investigate and obtain business credit and funding before they really need it. This credit can be grown to even greater amounts over time and can be secured without a personal guarantee. Now when a business owner runs into a BIG problem, they have the financial solution available.

Most business owners go to their bank when they need money. As many entrepreneurs are now discovering, banks have greatly tightened up their lending guidelines making it harder than ever to be approved. This is one of the main reasons that a business owner should check for financing with a company that offers multiple finance options.

The truth is there are billions of dollars ready to lend right now for small businesses. But much of the available funding cannot be secured through a conventional bank. Factoring companies, credit unions, merchant companies, private and angel investors all have money to lend to you right now.

But if a business owner doesn't exactly know what type of financing they need, it is tough to know where to look. For example, most business owners don't know about Business Revenue lending, or Purchase Order or Account Receivable Financing, or Equipment lease backs or merchant advances.

Most banks do not offer these types of financing options. And unless a business owner knows exactly the type of financing they are looking for, they will not know these options exist. Having access to finance options allows a business owner to obtain funding based on the strengths of their business, giving them a significantly greater chance of being approved.

Types of Available Credit and Funding

There are hundreds of financial products that are designed for businesses. Unfortunately, most businesses don't know about these products, only about the ones offered at their personal bank.

Most banks only offer SBA-insured loans. This means the only business loan products they offer require full documentation from the business owner, including financials, profit and loss statements, bank account statements, tax returns for 2-3 years, good personal credit from the business owner, and good personal credit.

If a business doesn't have all these things, most banks won't approve them. And even when a business does supply all these documents, they must be perfect, and show little or no issues, for the business to be approved. So, if there is an NSF on a bank statement, or one year doesn't show a lot of net profit, the business might be declined for most business funding programs.

Even though conventional banks don't offer many other financial products other than SBA loans, there are still many other forms of funding available for businesses that are not offered through banks. Many of these programs don't require all the financials and documentation that full document SBA programs require.

Many of these funding programs are easier to qualify for as they don't have all the stringent documentation requirements. Some funding programs even focus on one single aspect of the business and use that one aspect as collateral for the funding. For example, with a merchant advance the lender only looks at merchant statements. So, if the business does good credit card sales, the business can be approved for funding, even if the business owner's financials and personal credit are not good.

There are a lot of available funding programs. In this chapter we will discuss many of these programs that you might not have heard of before. Knowing these programs exist is the very important first step towards being able to apply and be approved.

Credit Lines

Unsecured revolving business credit lines are a smart way to grow and expand a business. The business owner pays only on the credit they use, making revolving credit lines a perfect financing source for most businesses. Plus, revolving business lines can be used, paid down, and then reused making them very practical for business owners. Knowing that additional money is available if needed gives tremendous peace of mind.

The amount a business will be approved for will vary depending on the volume of business being done. A business owner can secure a revolving credit line for over $150,000 with no financials needed to qualify, and credit lines up to $250,000 if they are willing to show their business tax returns and financials.

Some revolving lines require collateral be put up to qualify. Collateral can include accounts receivables, inventory, machinery & equipment, and even real estate. Other credit lines are available with limited to no financial documents needed to qualify.

Most business revolving credit lines require a personal guarantor to be approved. This means that if the business owner fails to meet the terms of the agreement, they will be personally liable. The business owner's personal credit will typically be used to qualify them for revolving business credit lines. A business can also qualify with a strong business credit profile and score built without the owner needing to provide a personal guarantee.

Most banks have cut back dramatically on the funds they are offering to small business owners. As a result, many owners have found it very difficult to obtain revolving business credit lines.

Brand new startup businesses with no financials can qualify for a credit line up to $150,000. There are no financials required for many of these types of credit lines and the lender won't even look at the business's monthly revenue. Most lenders want a strong business or personal credit profile for these types of credit lines.

If the business doesn't have a score and credit profile built, the lenders will want to look at the personal credit and will require the business owner to supply a personal guarantee. If a strong business credit profile and score are built, the business can then qualify on its own for these types of credit lines and the business owner can be approved with no personal guarantee. The better the personal or business credit is, the higher amount the credit line approval will be.

With most of these credit lines, the business owner can even use someone as a Personal Guarantor who does have good credit if that owner has credit issues now. A personal guarantor is someone who offers to be personally liable in case that debt is not paid. So, if a business owner has a friend sign as the personal guarantor, that friend would be liable if that debt was not paid. That would mean the lender could pursue the personal assets of that friend to get paid back in case the business owner defaulted on payments of the credit line.

Most anyone can be a personal guarantor. They do not usually need to be an owner of the business or even associated with the business. They only really need to have good credit and be willing to be liable in case the payments are not paid. Many business owners find personal guarantors from their friends, business partners, even family.

These credit lines are some of the best accounts in the country for new startup businesses and new franchises as they don't need any financials to qualify. These credit lines are revolving and can be used for almost any purpose. The business owner will receive a debit card, even a checkbook so they can write from this account. It only takes 2-4 weeks to close and have the money in their bank account.

Equipment Financing

One of the best and smartest ways to obtain the equipment for a business is by using Equipment Financing. A business owner can deduct the interest paid on the lease and not need a large down payment to be approved. This is one of the reasons over 80% of U.S. businesses use equipment lease financing to acquire equipment for their businesses.

Using Equipment Financing a business owner can improve business cash flow and increase capital. They can keep their normal cash flow, leave their money in the bank, avoid major out-of-pocket expenses incurred by purchasing the equipment up-front, and benefit from multiple tax advantages.

Equipment Leasing is one of the most common types of equipment financing available today. When leasing equipment, a business owner will find most leasing options offer fixed-rate financing. This means the interest rate and payments will stay the same from month-to-month during the term of the lease.

Whether the business needs office equipment or large commercial equipment used for manufacturing, equipment financing is a perfect solution for the business. Equipment financing can also be used for someone who is just starting a new business which needs equipment to operate.

There is typically no down payment required on equipment leasing loans. The lender will collect 1-2 of the monthly payments upon approval. This amount of money required is usually equal to 3-7% of the total equipment cost.

The business owner will have low monthly payments available. And the payments can be tailored to fit the company's individual needs. Taxes and other charges such as installation charges into new equipment leases can be included. Equipment loans are perfect for any business owner looking to purchase equipment.

Merchant Cash Advance

A business owner can get money for their business quickly by borrowing against future credit card sales. This type of financing is known as Merchant Cash Advances. These loans use your past and current credit card history to determine how much financing a business can be approved for.

Money is advanced to you based on how much the business processes each month in credit card transactions. Then a small portion of each future credit card sale goes towards paying back the merchant advance loan, not interfering with your cash and check receipts

There are no fixed repayment amounts or terms which gives flexibility to the business if it's having a slow month. One of the best benefits of merchant advances is that the business can receive money in its bank account as soon as 24 hours after approval.

Another great benefit of a merchant loan is that the business owner doesn't have to have good credit to qualify. These loans leverage positive credit card processing history for approval, not business owner personal credit scores. There are some credit score restrictions, but in most cases a business can be approved with even below average personal credit scores.

And there is no personal guarantee required and no collateral is needed.

Merchant loans can be obtained up to $150,000. How much a business will be approved for will be determined based on how much they process in credit card transactions each month.

Every business has its strengths and weaknesses. If a business uses credit cards as a payment source for clients, a merchant advance can be the perfect way for that business to obtain a lot of money in a short period of time. These loans are available for businesses that process as low as $3,500 monthly in credit card transactions. And the higher the processing volume the higher advance loan the business will be approved for.

There are no application fees and no out-of-pocket costs. And funds can be used for any purpose, including payroll, marketing, increasing business inventory, paying taxes, paying rent, advertising, ordering supplies and equipment, expanding the business and opening an additional location, or using the funds for working capital.

SBA Financing

One SBA program that might be perfect for many businesses is known as CAPLines. This is an umbrella loan program that helps small businesses meet their short-term and cyclical working-capital needs. There are many types of CAPLine types of lines-of-credit, including Seasonal lines, Contract lines, Builder lines, and Standard and Small Asset-Based lines.

Each line has a separate purpose that can help you and your business. For example, the Standard line is a revolving line-of-credit for cyclical growth, recurring, and short-term needs. The Seasonal lines can be used to offset lower revenues in slower seasons, while the contract lines can be used to pay for contract costs for expansion.

The SBA also has a great loan program called The Microloan Program. Although the name is Micro, the benefits to the business owner can be huge. The Microloan Program provides small, short-term loans to small businesses. Micro loans can provide working capital and fulfill other purposes when a business owner needs money the most.

Some of the common uses for Micro loans include working capital, the purchase of inventory or supplies, the purchase of furniture or fixtures, and the purchase of machinery or equipment. Terms, Interest Rates, and Fees and loan terms vary based on the size of the loan, the planned use of funds, the requirements of the intermediary lender, and the needs of the small business borrower.

Small Business 7(a) loans are well known and loved in the business community. If a business is awarded a 7(a) loan, the loan proceeds may be used to establish a new business or to assist in the acquisition, operation, or expansion of an existing business.

Directly from the SBA, here are some of the uses for loan proceeds:

- The purchase land or buildings, to cover new construction as well as expansion or conversion of existing facilities
- The purchase of equipment, machinery, furniture, fixtures, supplies, or materials
- Long-term working capital, including the payment of accounts payable and/or the purchase of inventory
- Short-term working capital needs, including seasonal financing, contract performance, construction financing and export production
- Financing against existing inventory and receivables
- The refinancing of existing business indebtedness that is not already structured with reasonable terms and conditions
- To purchase an existing business

The SBA has decided to give our veterans and military members some great funding incentives and special programs. One of the SBA programs is the SBA's Patriot Express program. This pilot Loan Initiative is for veterans and members of the military community wanting to establish or expand small businesses.

The SBA and its resource partners are further focusing extra efforts on counseling and training to augment this loan initiative, making it more accessible and easier to use.

Eligible military community members include:

- Veterans
- Service-disabled veterans
- Active-duty service members eligible for the military's Transition Assistance Program
- Reservists and National Guard members
- Current spouses of any of the above
- The widowed spouse of a service member or veteran who died during service or of a service-connected disability

Loans can be used for many purposes. Some of the most common purposes are:

- Start-up costs
- Equipment purchases
- Business-occupied real-estate purchases
- Inventory
- Infusing working capital
- Managing your business
- Expansion
- Preparing your business for the possibility of your deployment
- Setting up to sell goods and services to the government
- Recovery from declared disasters.

Patriot Express loans feature the SBA's lowest interest rates for business loans, generally 2.25 percent to 4.75 percent over prime depending upon the size and maturity of the loan

The Small Business Administration has an Express program to expedite loan approvals. The SBA *Express* program gives small business borrowers an accelerated turnaround time for the SBA to review the loan application. Applications can be approved within only 36 hours. In addition, lower interest rates are often available to you when your application is submitted through this VIP *Express* program.

Purchase Order Financing

Seasonal sales, business growth and expansion, and large orders can all restrict a business' cash flow. Many consumers want to pay on terms of net 30 or 60, but many suppliers demand payment on delivery.

At the same time the business has to cover other expenses, including shipping, labor costs, materials, packing and many more, further restricting cash flow. Purchase order financing helps free up business cash flow so the business can grow, and profits can soar.

A business can obtain funds based on outstanding purchase orders with existing clients. While a bank looks at the company's finances, these loans focus on the financing and credit of the business's customers. This means this type of financing can be obtained even if the business owner has damage to their personal or business credit profiles.

There are a few different types of Purchase Order Financing currently available. One currently available option is to obtain funds that are paid directly to your suppliers. A business owner can receive advances up to 100% of the purchase cost to their supplier. The bank will then pay the supplier and the business owner receives immediate access to your goods.

The bank will collect the invoice payments from the client and will also pay the balance between the order value and the amount paid to the supplier. The business owner receives the net total minus any fees once payment has been received.

A second purchase order financing option is to issue a letter of credit to the business suppliers. This letter is a commitment to pay the supplier on their fulfillment of certain conditions. The conditions are normally related to the supplier providing necessary documentation. These Letter of Credits are also governed by the regulations of the International Chamber of Commerce.

A third option is a Supplier Guarantee. This is a commitment to pay the supplier from the availability generated on the funding of the receivables when generated relating to the purchase transaction.

The amount of purchase order financing available for a business will depend on the volume of outstanding purchase orders they have. It is very practical to obtain over $500,000 in financing if the business has that amount or greater in orders. Some purchase order financing climbs as high as $20,000,000 or higher in funding. Funds can commonly be delivered within a week after approval, and interest rates and terms are typically very good.

Revenue Lending

A great way for businesses to access money is through revenue-based financing, sometimes referred to as revenue participation or revenue sharing funding. Revenue financing is a loan to a company which is paid back through a royalty on the revenues. Typically, this royalty is in the 2 to 5% range.

With revenue-based capital, instead of selling ownership in the company the owner sell rights to a percentage of the business' revenue for some period of time. Funding is commonly available up to 25% of a company's annual revenue. Money is received monthly, sometimes equal to 10% of monthly revenues. To qualify a company must have current revenue.

One of the benefits of revenue funding is that it provides a variable payment. If revenue for the business goes down, the loan payment also goes down equivalent. This is extremely helpful in seasonal industries.

Another difference compared to a bank is that lenders want a personal guarantee and collateral with most loans. Revenue based financing typically has no collateral requirement. Unlike bank loans there are also no personal guarantee requirements for the founder. This funding can be used for many purposes including growth capital. And there are no restrictive covenants.

Inventory Financing

Inventory financing is a bank line of credit secured by the company's inventory as collateral. With inventory financing, the borrower receives a loan in order to purchase inventory. The purchased inventory is then used as collateral against the loan.

This is a great finance option for business owners as it provides the inventory that a business needs without tying up cash, receivables, credit cards, or bank lines. This type of financing can help to free up some of the cash you have tied up in inventory for more pressing needs.

Inventory loans are perfect for businesses that enjoy a high inventory turnover rate but are short of the cash needed to replenish their supplies. These loans free up much-needed cash.

Inventory financing loans are also convenient for businesses that need to keep some capital free for other interests and investments. Lenders will typically need to see that a business has a proven sales history to get approved. And they will require the business to possess tangible inventory.

Lenders will want to see that the business has a proper inventory management system in place which provides accurate and timely information on your inventory size and cost. To get approved a business owner should ensure that the inventory is protected from damage and shrinkage. Most lenders will also require sales orders to verify the business is actually and actively selling.

401k Financing

Business partners can borrower against their 401ks to obtain funds for their business. To start setting up 401k financing a business will first adopt a retirement plan. Specifically, the retirement plan should be a profit-sharing plan that allows 100 percent of the plan assets attributable to rollovers to be invested in employer stock.

A 401(k) works perfect for Retirement plan financing. A business owner can quickly and easily rollover their retirement funds from their previous employer or IRA into the new 401(k) plan. The funds can come from multiple different sources and multiple people, including their spouse or an employee who is looking for an investment opportunity.

And, thanks to provisions in the tax code, this can be done without a penalty. By rolling funds into retirement financing the owner can buy a small business or use funds for their existing business and use these funds as an investment inside their retirement plan, without distribution penalties.

A few of the many benefits of Retirement Financing include:

- Utilize funds from retirement accounts like IRAs, 401(k)s, 403(b)s, Keoghs, SEPs, etc., without incurring early distribution taxes or penalties
- Start a small business with minimal to no debt while securing significant tax benefits
- Use up to 100% of retirement funds, or use a portion as a down payment on an SBA or unsecured loan
- Combine retirement funds with the retirement funds of a business partner or spouse
- Save thousands in interest fees and protect personal credit
- Lower business overhead while aggressively growing the business owner's retirement account

Wrap Financing

Wrap Financing is for business owners who want to "wrap" their vehicle with graphics. You have more than likely seen a wrapped vehicle before, and you might even be thinking about wrapping one of your vehicles now. Wrapping a vehicle turns it into a mobile billboard. Everywhere you go your car is advertising your business.

Many business owners swear by this marketing technique and insist it brings them significant amounts of business. But most business owners don't know that they can obtain financing to wrap their vehicles or even the windows in their business.

Wrapping a vehicle sometimes costs upwards of $2,500. But with financing available this makes it much more affordable for business owners.

Securities Based Loans

Securities Based Loans are an excellent source of funds for someone who holds publicly traded stocks. Securities-based lending is generally involving a revolving line of credit that uses eligible investment portfolio as collateral.

This funding option permits a business owner to access funds without immediately liquidating their portfolio. This gives them the ability to access liquidity while maintaining their portfolio's current exposure to the market. The business owner will continue to receive the benefit of any dividends, interest or capital appreciation that may accrue in the account.

Some of the other main benefits of securities financing include:

- Interest rates range from 2.5% to 4.5%, fixed, interest-only payments
- Loan periods up to 10 years
- Loans are NON-recourse, and not recorded
- Borrower retains full beneficial interest (dividends, appreciation, etc.)
- Funds may be used for virtually any purpose, anywhere in the world
- Borrower's nationality and residence can be anywhere in the world

This is a non-recourse; non-recorded loan and the lender cannot come after you personally nor report you to the credit bureaus in case of non-payment. So, if the business owner defaults, they get to keep the money, and the lender gets to keep the stock as the sole remedy.

At the end of the loan period, the borrower will receive back from the lender the same number of shares originally pledged as collateral, which automatically includes any appreciation as well. This is a great option for many business owners, especially foreign nationals, borrowers with limited or undocumented income, and there is no credit check, so you qualify even with challenged credit.

Signage Financing

Commercial signage can be expensive. To have a company install a sign in front of your business, especially a lighted sign, can cost thousands of dollars.

Many companies skimp on their signage due to the huge cost of commercial signage. But business owners do have the ability to finance their signage insuring they can afford the best signage available. Now that business can stand out and attract more clients.

Private Investors

There are a lot of private investors who are currently hungry to invest money into make-sense projects. These investors will gladly offer loans for many projects when most banks won't. This gives a business owner a great opportunity to secure the money they need to grow their business, even if their bank has said no.

Receivables Financing

Receivables Financing or "invoice factoring" is a great way to get money for a business. Accounts receivable financing is not a loan; it's an advance against client invoices. The business is selling outstanding invoices to a factoring company who then gives back up to 95% of the invoice value in the form of a loan against those invoices.

Receivable Financing is mainly used to generate immediate cash flow for the business selling the accounts receivable. These are a great funding option as they provide an immediate advance of cash to a business leveraging its outstanding invoices. This means that as the business grows, so does the amount of funding the business will qualify for so it can meet increasing demand. This is why most major companies including most major Fortune 500 companies use some form of Accounts Receivable Financing.

One of the best benefits of receivable financing is that the business receives an increase in working capital without needing to borrow money or tie up business or personal assets. This boost to cash flows positively impacts profitability. Money can be received quickly, typically within 24 hours from approval. This is much faster than if the business was trying to collect on the invoices on its own and wait for that money.

Prior to purchasing invoices, a factor conducts a credit analysis on the client being invoiced to determine their risk or repaying the invoice. The business owner is then entitled to the resulting analysis, which is a huge benefit as it can assist the business owner in their future business dealings with that client.

Another big benefit of Receivable Financing is that the business is not obtaining a loan. The cash advanced is based on the client's credit status, not the business owner holding the receivables, making it easier to qualify for.

A business may qualify for factoring even if they are a new company without an established track record, have a tax lien, or have even declared bankruptcy. This is not considered a loan since the business is literally selling its own receivables. A business can be approved for as much as 25 million dollars in financing.

Accounts Receivable Financing really boosts cash flow by providing an immediate advance of cash into the business against the value of the business's outstanding invoices.

Angel investors can be your saving grace when a business is looking for business funding. Sometimes angel investors are willing to lend money when other banks and financial institutions simply won't. Interest rates and fees with angel investors can also be very favorable, sometimes better than bank rates and terms.

Even though angel investors are a great source of business funding, there are some things to be cautious about before committing with an investor. Despite their name, angel investors are not there to rescue the business. These investors are usually businesses or individuals who have money to lend but expect to take a safe risk and earn a nice return on their investment.

These investors are usually one-time investors. Many angel investors do not lend to the same person twice, even if that person paid them back perfectly. They choose to spread their risk out over many people and many businesses to insure they get a safe return on their investment.

Another concern with angel investors is that they typically want a percentage or part of the company to lend the money. Sometimes they want a small stake, and other times they want full control and 51% ownership. But in most cases, they do want a percentage of the company itself.

When the investor does want a stake in the company it is important that the terms are acceptable for the business owner as well. The investor's funds can really help grow a business, but the trade-off of handing over part of the company means the deal has to be worth it for the business owner as well as the angel investor.

Another concern with angel investors is that they sometimes commit but don't follow through and close on the transaction. For this reason, it is essential that the business owner does not spend any of the funds until the deal is completely done, and the funds are in the bank. Nothing is worse than committing those funds only to discover that the deal falls apart and the angel investor never delivers the funds.

Angel investors are a great source of money for your business. But make sure you watch out and make the best decisions for you and your business if moving forward with this type of investor.

Private Equity

Private equity financing is money that is invested in a privately held business in exchange for partial ownership of the business. The invested funds might come from private individuals or institutional investors. Regardless of where it comes from, there are many individuals and businesses that are ready and willing to invest in a make-sense business.

The goal of the investment is to earn more of a rate-of-return than could be earned otherwise. It can be like venture capital or angel investors where the investors can choose to invest in start-up funding, but usually the business has been operating for a while and needs money for expansion.

Private equity financing often involves large amounts of capital even though there is no set limit of how low or high the investment can be. Despite the fluid nature of this type of financing, there are criteria a business will have to meet in order to obtain this type of business funding.

The investors will look for assurances that their money will be used wisely and in a way that increases the likelihood that the investment will bring higher returns than would be expected if giving business loans.

The investor will balance the risk of investment loss again the possibility of investment gains and then decide as to whether the risk is manageable and makes sense.

The investor will look to see if the entrepreneur assumes more risk exposure than the equity partners or investors, what stage the business is currently at in a startup or well-established business looking to expand, how much experience the management has in the industry, is the size of the investment request and how it compares to the size of the business.

The investor will also look to see if there is a quality business plan with realistic goals and projections, to see if there is a marketing plan complete, look to see what is the company's history including its historical financial and market performance, and to see if the business is willing to accept investor restrictions placed on the investment.

The last question may seem obvious at first glance, but it's on the list for a reason. Private equity investors can set their own unique requirements and restrictions for business funding, and you must be willing to agree to them. The good news though is that you have more negotiating leeway since this is private funding and not financial institution lending.

Though companies have been experiencing difficulties getting approved for business loans in the current economy, private equity financing has always been available. Unfortunately, many business owners simply don't know how to go about finding or raising this type of money. There are many sources of capital available today ranging from angel investors to private equity financing.

Crowd Funding

Crowd funding is a great financing source for new startup businesses that have a limited budget. Crowd funding is the process of getting funding from a community instead of an individual or finance institution. The network pools their money and resources to support the new business.

If someone is starting a business, they can post their project idea to the community. If the community sees your project and idea as promising, they give out the necessary funding, without any interests or collateral. Crowd funding enables the small guys with big ideas to be able to secure funding to start their endeavor.

Crowd funding originally started as a way to help generate funds for charities. It then became popular for artists, including street performers, before becoming a viable funding option for other small businesses. In 1997 the British band Marillion even funded their entire tour through crowd funding. So, since its original inception this funding vehicle has been used for a very diverse group of entrepreneurs.

Crowd funding is similar to angel investing as investors don't require any principals returned or interests paid. With some crowd funding the business owner can even offer something in return for their supporters' money. Millions of supporters are active in crowd funding communities with money to lend.

The average loan amount is smaller. On average loan amounts are below $25,000, and in many cases, loans are for even smaller amounts of $5,000-10,000. Crowd funding is perfect for entrepreneurs who don't have a standard business model that fits with normal funding. It is also perfect for new business owners who have great ideas and only need a little money to get going.

Credit Cards

As a small business owner, it can be quite a challenge deciding which is the best business credit card for the business owner and the business. When looking for the best types of card for the business, an owner will first want to know about the different types of business credit cards that are available today.

A Business Debit Card is a card that works like a business checkbook because the limit is the amount of funds the business currently has available in its business checking account. Every time the card is used it to make a purchase the amount charged is deducted right from that account.

A Prepaid Business Card is a convenient alternative to carrying cash and works just like a secured consumer credit card. Funds are added to the account and whatever amount is added is available to use for purchases.

A Secured Business Credit Card is specifically designed for businesses with no credit or less than perfect credit history. An initial security deposit is required which establishes the card's credit limit. In most cases a minimum deposit of $500 is required and once the business owner begins making purchases, they will receive invoices like a regular credit card.

An Unsecured Business Credit Card works just like a normal, revolving, unsecured consumer credit card. Credit limits are based upon many factors, depending on the issuer and can range from personal credit and/or business credit ratings, years in business, annual revenues and so on. These credit cards give the business the opportunity to earn incentives and rewards.

A Business Charge Card has all the convenience of a credit card without the high interest rates.

When using this card, the business owner will have to pay the card balance in full each billing cycle. Because they can't carry a balance, a charge card doesn't have a periodic or annual percentage rate, so there is no rate for a charge card issuer to disclose.

If the owner plans on paying the balance off each month, a card offering travel mile rewards or cash back bonuses may be the best business credit cards. If on the other hand they plan on maintaining an ongoing balance, a low introductory or standard APR might be a better option.

Remember, just because a card issuer offers all kinds of perks and rewards doesn't mean it's necessarily the best card. A business owner should always read the fine print to completely understand the terms and conditions and fees associated with the card.

It's also important to note that even though business credit cards are not covered under the new CARD Act certain issuers are extending the CARD Act protections to its card holders. This is just another factor to consider when applying for a business credit card for a business.

Understanding Personal Credit

This book covers a lot of information about how to build business credit for a business. But this book wouldn't be complete unless it included a chapter also covering how personal credit works. This is essential, as it helps you better understand business credit, and personal credit will play an important role for any business that is applying for funding.

A lot of business credit sources will approve a business with no personal credit check. This means a business can secure a lot of credit, including store credit cards and other credit from Visa, MasterCard, even American Express.

But most funding which includes loans, credit lines, even merchant advances will require some kind of credit check from the lender. In most of those cases the lender doesn't make the lending decision based on the personal credit. They are mainly looking at the personal credit to ensure the business owner isn't currently having financial issues.

Your Credit Quality of Life

It is easier to understand business credit fundamentals when you have a good background of what credit is, and how the consumer credit system works. Credit is defined as an agreement between a creditor or lender and a borrower in which the consumer assumes something of value in an agreement to repay the creditor, based on certain terms.

Car dealers, banks, credit card companies, mortgage companies, signature loan companies, pay day advances, even student loan agencies, are a few of many sources who extend credit to individuals.

When a person goes to apply for new credit, these creditors review the credit profile to determine the individual's risk of repaying that debt. Based on their risk they might get approved or denied.

If they do get approved, the repayment terms will again be based on the quality of their credit profile. The better the credit profile and the higher the consumer score, the better terms the borrower will receive.

When a consumer's credit profile is damaged, they will be charged higher interest based on that risk. The rate of interest will vary based on many factors, but interest charges can be significant. One credit card company in 2009 even released a credit card with an 89% APR!

Importance of Credit

Your life is your credit. If you have ever been denied a loan or even a job due to your credit, then you already know the importance your credit profile has to your life.

Most of the payments an individual pays each month are affected by their credit quality. Home loans, rent, car payments, credit cards, installment loans, car insurance, cell phones, health and life insurance, and even monthly utilities are all based on the quality of a consumer's personal credit.

From the payments a consumer pays each month, to whether they rent or own their dream home are based solely on their credit quality. New employers are even relying on credit to help make hiring decisions. It is impossible to hide from your credit. And as more companies rely on it to gauge risk, the importance of having a good, solid, consumer credit profile is ever increasing.

But credit is also very scary. Most consumers don't know how credit works or even what that magical credit score really means. One thing is for sure, there is a dramatic difference in quality of life between having bad or good credit.

Life with Bad Credit

A person can live with credit issues. But every year those issues will cost the consumer tens of thousands of dollars, making it hard to survive and near impossible to save money for their future.

This is one of the fundamental reasons the United States savings rate has stayed under 1% for four years through 2007. Many consumers don't have the extra money to save due to paying tens of thousands of dollars each year in outlandish interest charges.

I have spent over eleven years in the finance industry. During this time, I have done thousands of financial reviews with clients and most of my clients had no idea how much their credit was really costing them.

Sure, they knew that bad credit was causing issues with them getting approved for new credit. But, my clients, like most consumers, never REALLY know how much credit affects their day to day lives.

Bad credit ruins lives. This is one of the most shocking but REAL statements you might read in a while. The difference between living life and struggling to survive is based completely on credit quality.

Let's look at a car as a simple example. Most people in today's society need a vehicle to get around. We require one to get to our jobs, our kids to day care, or just to get to the store. There are an estimated 250 million car owners in the U.S. alone, so chances are pretty good you are one of them or know someone who is.

Many car owners chose to finance their vehicles and pay monthly payments until the debt is paid off. Car loans are offered to consumers based on their credit history and their credit scores, like most other loans.

And based on those credit factors, risk will be determined by the auto lender and an interest rate will be established for the consumer to pay back that loan. The payments will then be established based on the loan amount, interest rate, and term of the loan.

With good credit, a consumer will get approved for a longer term and better interest rate. With bad credit, they will pay much greater interest on a shorter term, making your payments much higher.

Okay, so maybe you already knew all that. Many consumers do, but most don't know how much that extra interest and shorter terms is really costing them.

A $20,000 car loan with good credit will cost approximately $322 monthly. This is based on a 5% interest rate for 72 months. The exact same $20,000 car loan with bad credit will cost approximately $541 monthly. This is based on a 21% interest rate for 60 months.

This is the same car, but one is costing $219 more EVERY month. The person with good credit will pay $23,184 for their car. The consumer with bad credit will pay $32,460 for the same car. That's a $9,276 difference. This means the same car will cost the consumer with bad credit 46% more than the one with good credit.

These examples are not extreme. These are based on common interest rates a consumer will actually see on a $20,000 auto loan. Rent and home expenses are another area where customers get taken for great amounts of interest.

A $100,000 mortgage costs a good credit consumer $577 monthly and $207,720 over 30 years. The same home would cost a family with challenged credit $841 monthly and $302,760 over 30 years.

The consumer with good credit will pay $264 less per month and save $95,040 over the lifetime of the loan. That means the person with bad credit will pay $95,040 more in interest for a $100,000 loan, due to their credit.

Credit cards might cost $116 more monthly based on credit. Utility payments are higher, insurance payments are more, and so are many other regular family expenses.

Most people know credit has an adverse effect on their life. But the truth is, bad credit controls their lives. Outrageous amounts of extra interest are being charged each and every month. That debt and those higher payments strap most families, forcing them to live paycheck-to-paycheck.

If even one emergency arises, many consumers in this position are susceptible to a total financial catastrophe. With bad credit, their lives are just like a house of cards waiting to collapse.

Consumers with credit issues don't have high open limits to use in case of emergencies. When a transmission goes out or a child needs emergency dental treatment, payday loans become about the only option to get money in a pinch. The rates on those are extremely high, making them almost impossible to pay off.

Life is tough with bad credit, really tough. With no available credit, one emergency can wipe you out. And there is no extra money each month, due to hundreds-of-dollars each month spent on excessive interest charges.

Many then are so caught up with financial survival that they forget about how innocently it all began. Instead, they are caught in a trap which few actually recover from.

The Bad Credit Trap

I call this the Bad Credit Trap. This is a trap most consumers will never get out of. The system won't allow them to naturally recover.

In my career, I have heard thousands of clients tell me how good their credit was before it went bad. But I have never had even one client with good credit tell me their credit was bad and it magically got better.

Most with bad credit never recover. That is a fact. And the reason is that the system is against them from the start. Consumers with credit issues are not in their situations because they are bad people. They are sucked into a trap that most simply don't know how to recover from.

Credit problems usually stem from an uncontrollable event. Some have a car crash or medical issue that compiles medical bills. Many others go through divorce or have credit too young, leading to issues where a default or late payment occurs.

There are thousands of reasons things happen, but let's just say life happens. And when life happens, and even one account gets paid late, a downward credit spiral then begins. Even if the late payment was for one credit card, most other card companies will claim their risk is higher.

Several things start to happen at this point. First, many creditors will lower their limits. If a creditor lowers the high credit limit on an account, the credit score always goes down. This is due to 1/3 of your credit score being based on your Available Credit

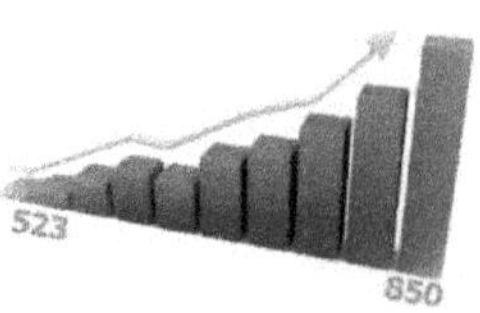

Now the consumer has less available credit, right when they obviously need it. Plus, with lower available credit, they will face more overdraft fees. And the credit scores drop, and risk increases for all other accounts, due to the lower score.

Now creditors will start to increase interest rates due to the increased risk. Not all creditors can do this, but in the fine print, many reserves the right to do just that. The higher rates mean the payments also increase. The consumer is now faced with higher payments on several of their accounts, not to mention having to pay their original late fees.

Eventually, this leads to many consumers going late on other payments. Then things start to get really bad, really fast. In a very short period of time, credit that once was good is now left destroyed.

This means all new credit the consumer applies for will only be approved at high risk rates. This costs hundreds more dollars every month and radically deteriorates the consumer's quality of life, for many years to come.

Most consumers then continue to struggle all their life with this cycle. The high interest rates and payments leave them living paycheck-to-paycheck. And they commonly go late on their payments after that, as they struggle to pay outlandishly high interest rates and payments.

This is the Bad Credit Cycle. Many times, it starts with one unavoidable late payment. But in the end, it costs most any chance of having a healthy financial future.

Life with Good Credit

Life with good credit is an entirely different story. Many people believe they want to be rich, financially. But what many don't realize is that their fantasy life has less to do with being rich and more to do with having good credit.

Mercedes Benz is a great symbol of car luxury. Many people dream of having the opportunity to own one. In their dreams, they fantasize about being rich and driving a Mercedes. With good credit, a brand-new Mercedes Benz can cost as little as $326 monthly. Even a luxury home can be financed for less than $1,000 monthly.

The secret to wealth, in many cases, has less to do with being rich and more to do with credit quality. Even a crazy dream like walking into a store and buying whatever you want or buying a car on your credit can be reached if you have good credit, even if you are not wealthy.

Good credit won't stand in the way of getting a good job or getting approved for new credit at 0% interest rates. Good credit makes living the American dream of home ownership a reality. It even makes driving a Corvette or a Harley Davidson practical.

Credit lines are issued to consumers based on their credit quality. With good credit, it is common for consumers to receive credit lines and credit cards for $10,000 or higher. In many cases the interest on those cards is also less than 3%, making them ideal for many situations, especially emergencies. Good credit creates peace of mind for this reason.

Let me tell you a little lender secret here. Good credit clients in most businesses are treated better than those with credit issues. Auto dealers, banks, mortgage companies may try not to, but most do treat good credit customers as superior.

I don't agree with this at all, but I saw it every day of my eleven years in finance. Good credit customers are offered better deals than those with credit issues.

The main reason is that good credit buyers are stereotyped as smart, intellectual, educated, people who do their research and will leave in a minute if they think they are being taken advantage of. So, this fear has most sales managers coddling good credit prospects.

In today's society, good credit is like being rich. When you have it you are treated better, can spend more and pay less, and absolutely afford to have the life of your dreams.

Good credit is the hidden secret of life. And this secret to the credit system, secrets behind your credit scores, and even a proven secret system to correct your credit will be revealed in the following chapters.

A Consumer's Role in the Credit System

As important as credit is, most people sure hope that *someone* is ensuring your credit report reflects legitimate and accurate information. This is the common belief I have always heard from clients. They believe that someone, maybe the government, the bureaus, the creditors, but someone, is insuring that reported data is accurate and correct.

But the sad truth is, nobody is watching this for the consumer at all. As a consumer, you are the ONLY person involved with your credit who benefits from your credit profile being positive and accurate.

The credit bureaus, like many companies, do have to abide by certain federal and state laws. They are also required to investigate credit disputes based on certain criteria per laws like the Fair Credit Reporting Act. But the credit bureaus don't question what creditors report, unless they themselves are questioned on it.

Creditors also have to abide by state and federal laws. But most reporting creditors don't have divisions within their companies where they validate what they are reporting.

The credit bureaus and creditors do have one thing in common in regard to the reporting of your data. They both make more money the worse your credit is.

Every time you apply for new credit data is collected from you. The data is collected and then submitted to the credit bureau as an inquiry.

The inquiry comes back to the creditor as a credit file. Your credit file consists of information on your prior credit accounts, your credit score, and your residence and employment information.

This information is then used by the creditor to offer or deny you financing. In most cases, the creditor won't even let you have a copy of the report they are using. You have to order your own, making it even harder to ensure the data they are seeing is accurate.

But due to prior credit bureau abuse and misreporting of information, you are entitled to one free copy of your credit report each year. This is because the federal government is not monitoring your report for accuracy, but instead, they are depending on you to self-regulate your own credit profile.

You are expected to get a copy of your report each year to make sure it is accurate. When you do this, you will always want to check all the data very carefully on your report for accuracy. YOU are the ONLY person dealing with your credit who benefits by having an accurate and positive credit.

So, take it upon yourself to get a copy of your free report, dispute any inaccurate information, and manage your credit wisely. You are the only one who benefits when your profile is positive and accurate, don't forget this.

Credit Score Secrets Revealed

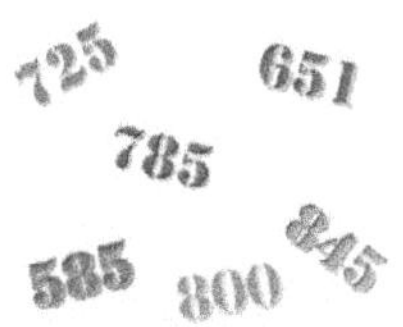

You are probably familiar with your credit score. Nowadays you can gain access to your credit reports and your credit scores much easier than in the past. This is because government regulations are now giving consumers more access to this once highly secretive credit system.

Knowing your credit score is important but knowing how your credit score works is essential. Once you know and understand the components of your credit score and how they work, you will then be able to make small adjustments and make radical increases to your scores.

The Credit Score Breakdown

There are many credit scorecards in existence today. But the underlying principal components of all those models remain the same. Some will rate certain aspects of your credit scores higher, but the scores themselves are built on the same five ingredients.

Payment History- 35%

Your payment history is the largest aspect of your credit score, as you might expect. In total, your pay history accounts for ***35%*** of your total score.

This aspect of your total score calculation is based on your prior payment history with your creditors. Late payments, defaulted accounts, bankruptcies, and all other negative information on your credit report have the greatest effect.

The more recent the late payment, the greater the damage is to your credit score. If you go late on your mortgage this month, the Mortgage Industry Option scoring model could drop your scores over 120 points. That is with only one 30-day late payment!

The scoring model is based on your potential to go 90 days late on an account within the next 2 years. Any recent late payments are a big reflection that you will default, and your credit score plummets as a result.

Your creditor cannot report you late unless you are 30 days late. But they will claim they need 10 days to process your payment. So, don't think that just because you mailed your payment on the 25th day that they will not report you late.

Altogether, your entire history of payment counts for 35% of your total scores. The more positive accounts you have and the less negative means a much higher credit score.

Percentage of High-Credit Used- 30%

The second largest factor in your credit scores is the amount you owe in relation to your high credit limits.

If you are carrying high credit card balances, you can actually hurt your credit scores almost as much as paying the account late every month. This is because if you go late, you affect 35% of your score, but if you use a high percentage of your available credit you affect 30% of your scores.

This is why we highly recommend to our clients that they get approved for new credit. We even help guide them to a large limit account, such as a $5,000 line-of-credit which requires no credit check. This high balance account will really open up the available credit on the report and increase the scores.

This aspect of your credit score has several different factors. The first factor is your relation of balances you owe on all of your accounts in relation to the high credit limits on those accounts. Once again, this takes into consideration balances on all of your accounts combined. Your credit score also considers balances in relation to high credit limits on your individual accounts.

For example, you will be scored higher if you owe 30% or less on your credit card accounts. This means if you have a high credit limit of $1,000, you will have a higher score if you maintain a balance of $300 or less.

For revolving accounts, such as credit cards, you want to keep the smallest balances while still keeping a balance. Don't pay the account to 0, and not use it. If you stop using the account, your credit score is not increasing. Pay it as close to 1% as you can, but make sure you keep your balances below 30%.

Your scores will also be lower due to higher balances on installment loans, car loans, mortgages, and other non-revolving accounts. This is why your credit scores will always be immediately lower if you open any of these accounts new.

A new car loan, for example, will lower your scores once it goes on your report. How much lower depends on your spread of other accounts.

As your loans and mortgages are paid down over time, your scores will steadily increase. This is why one of the best things you can do for your credit is open accounts and pay them as agreed. Don't pay those accounts to 0 too quickly, as you won't be getting credit for that account if you have no balance and no payments due.

Your score will be affected by how many open accounts of yours have balances, how much of your total credit lines are being used, and how much of a balance you have on installment loans, such as car loans. You can directly improve your credit scores by maintaining lower balances on your accounts or spreading balances over several different accounts. You can also get approved for new high-limit accounts to increase your scores.

Length of Credit History- 15%

Your "time in the bureau" accounts for 15% of your credit score. The older you are and the longer you have had credit accounts for, the higher the score. This is why it is near impossible to get to an 800 score at a young age. As you have more accounts throughout your life and your history grows over time, your scores will naturally increase due to this factor.

Being added as an authorized user to an account with a long pay history is another pay to increase your scores. Be careful how you do this. The new scoring models won't give you credit for most authorized user accounts unless they are family members of yours.

If you do have a family member who has had positive open accounts open for some time, see if they will add you as an authorized user on one of their accounts.

They have no risk, as you won't be able to use the account unless they physically give you a card. But you will get credit on your reports, and this will increase your credit scores.

Accumulation of New Debt- 10%

Accumulation of new debt accounts for 10% of your total credit score. This aspect of your credit score is comprised of how much new debt you are applying for. It takes into consideration how many accounts you currently have open, how long it has been since you opened a new account, and how many requests you have for new credit within a 12 month time period.

If you go out today and apply for credit, that creditor requests information from the credit bureaus. This counts as an inquiry on your report. If you have a lot of inquiries in a short period of time, your scores will be impacted.

If you apply for a mortgage today, your scores might drop one point. But, if you apply for a car, a mortgage, and a few credit cards this week, your scores could drop significantly. The same applies if you have twelve car dealers pull your credit, or if one dealer has twelve banks pull your credit. A lot of credit pulls in a short period of time will have a great impact on your scores.

Don't apply for too much new credit in a short period. And don't let a lot of different creditors pull your report while applying for big purchases. You should also monitor your credit report for inquiries and dispute any that you are not familiar with or feel should be removed.

Healthy Mix of Credit Accounts- 10%

Your credit scores consider the "mix" of credit items you have on your report. This part of your credit score is affected by what kinds of accounts you have and how many of each. The bureaus will score you higher if you have an open mortgage, 3 credit cards, 1 auto loan, and a small number of other open accounts.

If you have a ton of credit cards, your scores will be lowered. If you have several mortgages, your scores will be lower. Any "unhealthy" account mixes lower your scores. The preferred number of credit cards is three. This means you will actually have a higher credit score if you have three open credit cards than if you have more or less than three open.

Don't run out and cancel your cards just yet. Remember, 30% of your score is comprised of your balances in relation to your high credit limit. So, keep your cards open, but focus on having three large balance cards for maximum impact. Maintain a healthy mix of accounts and this aspect of your credit score will be golden.

There are many different credit scoring models available for creditors. But the underlying makeup of the score is consistent. Now you know exactly how your credit score works. With this information, you can make even minor adjustments to how you use credit and see a major increase to your scores.

The Final Words

Business credit allows a business to build credit and obtain funding without the business owner being personally liable for the debt. This is one of the biggest benefits and greatest driving factors for any business owner to want to build a strong business credit profile and score.

With a strong business credit profile built, a business can qualify for massive amounts of credit and funding. A business can secure store credit cards, Visa cards, MasterCard credit cards, even American Express cards.

A strong business credit profile also helps a business qualify for credit lines, loans, merchant advances, factoring, and many other sources of funding. Having access to large amounts of working capital is essential with helping the business grow into a healthy, profitable company.

Established business credit also adds value to the business. Any potential future sale of the business will greatly be benefited when the business has an already established positive business credit profile.

The stronger the profile, and more depth in trade lines, the more valuable the business becomes to investors and other parties who might be interested in purchasing the business in the future.

The business owner already has an established personal credit profile that can be leveraged for the business owner to be approved for credit and loans. With business credit established the business will have double the borrowing power as it will have access to the business credit, and the personal credit of the business owner.

Business credit can be used to obtain funding with no personal guarantee from the business owner, providing a major additional benefit when the business credit is being used instead of the business owner's personal credit.

A good business credit profile and score can be built much faster than a business owner can build their personal credit profile. And, business credit approvals tend to be higher dollar amounts than business owners see through personal credit approvals.

Credit limits on business credit accounts tend to be higher. It is easier and faster to get approved with multiple credit sources. Business credit offers incentives similar to those for consumer credit such as points and free gifts.

And it is easier to get approved for multiple credit cards or credit lines with individual business credit sources than it is with consumer credit approvals.

These are only some of the significant number of benefits that building business credit provides to a business and the business owner. For all these reasons, it is tough for any business to truly be successful without establishing a good business credit profile and score and leveraging that to help the business prosper.

You are now empowered with the knowledge and tools you need to ensure your business can obtain and maintain an excellent business credit profile and score. Put your knowledge to use today and get started on building business credit for your business, or using business credit to help you start a new business venture.

Once you have built a positive business credit profile, make sure you use all the tips in this book to keep grow your business credit and keep your credit profile good throughout the lifetime of your business. Once you do this, you can finally have the positive business credit and the financial future you deserve.

www.ingramcontent.com/pod-product-compliance
Ingram Content Group UK Ltd.
Pitfield, Milton Keynes, MK11 3LW, UK
UKHW051241300926
15471UKWH00015B/1486

9 798215 747131